Images and Self-Images

Images and Self-Images

Male and Female
in Morocco

DAISY HILSE DWYER

New York · Columbia University Press

Printed in the United States of America
Columbia University Press
New York   Guildford, Surrey

Library of Congress Cataloging in Publication Data

Dwyer, Daisy Hilse.
   Images and self-images.

   Bibliography: p.
   Includes index.
   1. Women (in religion, folklore, etc.)—Morocco.
2. Women—Morocco—Taroudannt.   3. (Women,
Muslim—Morocco—Taroudannt.   4.   Tales, Moroccan.
I.   Title.
GR353.3.D89   392′6′0964   77-27835
ISBN 0-231-04302-3
ISBN 0-231-04303-1 pbk.
10 9 8 7 6

CONTENTS

v

Contents

PREFACE

F or centuries in the West, the Arab-Muslim world has sustained a textured image of exoticism, decadence, power, and
romance. World of the "infidel," it housed Christianity's most
fervent opponents and provided one context for Europe's so-
called chivalrous age. Setting for the 1001 nights, it still continues
to evoke images of eunuch slaves and Salome-like ladies maneuvering in lush palaces. It induces awe and a certain degree of
discomfort as the earliest provider of "high culture," a region
which, as modern Arab-Muslims are apt to remind us, might rise
to world leadership again.

These and other associations draw the attention of the Westerner in part because each in itself provides its particular drama.
The Crusades scene has inspired numerous artistic masterpieces;
the 1001 nights' confrontation has its many romantic renditions;
the vying of the oil barons and the West's industrial moguls

appears continually on television and in the press. Religion, sex, and money, three great sources of solace and discord, take root at the heart of the West's Arab-Muslim fantasy.

Of the three, it is perhaps the sexual world that has most continually, albeit most gently, engaged the curiosity of Westerners. The religious crusade is largely done in the West's eyes, and the economic battle only recently has begun to address the average Western citizen directly. But everyone is acquainted with the outlines of the sexual world, and the Arab-Muslim–Western contrast sparks projections and queries on both sides.

It is thus not surprising that the question most immediately posed to a female anthropologist working in the Middle East or North Africa is likely to be: "What is it like for a Western woman to live in the Arab world?" The question betrays expectations of difficulty: the dilemma of veiling or not veiling, the issue of sexual discreteness or involvement, and the options of submission and protest quickly work their way into the Westerner's mind.

For this woman anthropologist, these questions pointed beyond a set of decisions to be made about life-style, toward the intricacies of a set of dialogues in which Arab-Muslim men and women engage. Veiling, non-veiling, sexual purity, submission, and protest as labels for behavior already carry images, many of them mistaken ones, which have rooted themselves in a Western– Arab-Muslim discourse and so have had an impact on both regions. But they also allude to the complex dialogues which occur between Arab-Muslim men and women as they interact, male-male, male-female, female-female. There are different cover terms and meanings for these practices on the Arab-Muslim side, but similar questions are implied once these are pinpointed: what is the meaning of veiling, virginity, saintliness, and a host of other concepts that are or seem to be key to Arab-Muslim male-female relations; when and why do men and women take part in acting these patterns out; what do the two sexes feel about them and about themselves as they enact them?

These questions imply confrontation with a political phenomenon that the Westerner judges to be blatant in the Arab-Muslim world and that, one might add, certain Arab-Muslims perceive to be blatant in the West: the subordination of women. My task in this volume is to take a hard look at this phenomenon and matters associated with it: to lay bare the blindnesses (why, for example, do so few Westerners ask the male anthropologist what it is like for a Western man to live in the Arab-Muslim world?), to delineate a working focus (the structure and functioning of male dominance and female subordination might serve as a better starting point), and to determine the contributing parts of the system so as to lay the groundwork for symbolic analysis.

The last, ultimate goal implies a difficult task, for meaning lies in the unconscious as well as the conscious part of mind and behavior. The methodological dilemma thus asserts itself strongly: how can one discover how people perceive themselves and their behavior, in this case in the realm of male-female relations in one Muslim society that takes itself to be predominantly Arab? Since it is the many levels of meaning in an ultimately political discourse that fascinate, I have gravitated to the data provided by the various discourses in which Arab-Muslim men and women engage as they consider or confront maleness, femaleness, and sexuality: conversation, ritual, document, aphorisms, proverbs, and folklore.

Of these materials, the southern Moroccan folktales particularly intrigued me and so became the chief data base for this volume. Straightforward in their ideological messages and to the point in their action, they can be called moral tales, for they convey unambiguous messages about good and evil, human nature, injustice, and proper human priorities in life. Most can also be called sexual tales, for male-female interaction forms the chief component in the majority of them. Indeed, it is partly through the interaction of male and female characters that the Moroccan listener learns what maleness and femaleness are about and the feelings that he or she should have in response. Parsimonious, trenchant, and "without a doubt . . . on the first rung of the oral literatures of the entire world" (Lacoste-Dujardin 1973: 249), the Moroccan tales have an artfulness that renders their sexual-moral content clear and compelling.

Moroccan folk moral tales implicitly and explicitly educate their listeners in the belief and control systems that help maintain male dominance and female subordination in Morocco. Adults who wish to underscore certain points about male and female for children or guests are apt to glide into folktales at strategic times in the course of conversation. The phrase *gal li-k* (literally "he said it to you") augurs a moral tale much as it might promise the telling of an insightful real-life episode. Or more formal folktelling sessions might provide occasions for defining and projecting the recounter's wisdom about sexual politics. After sunset, a group of women and children might gather in one of their houses, their menfolk more rarely among them. First, they eat and converse; then each adult tells a tale, about male-female relations or not, until all have recited. At first, the youngest children merely listen. Soon, however, they make their first attempts at recitation while their parents laboriously correct them, until such time as they can reproduce adult content and style.

While folktelling is an important educative device among women, it also engages men in certain male-female or male-male interactions. Men might gather amicably to tell tales and gossip in the neighborhood coffeehouses, in stores, or in their gardens. One of the male folktellers who contributed substantially to the sexual-moral tales in this volume reported that he greatly augmented his repertoire while working in the desert. He said that he and his helper passed many an evening without family telling each other tales.

The folktelling session, like conversational folktelling, tends particularly to evoke tales from those men and women who have been less directly affected by a Western way of life. Older men and women tell their tales with pride, and listeners especially desire to hear such recitations. Moreover, older women, typically a conservative force in the male-female and other spheres, tend to be the least constrained conveyors of tales, for supernatural restrictions encumber all others. Persons who tell folktales before sunset are believed to sire or bear hairless children. The menopausal woman alone is free from this danger by virtue of her barrenness, and so can use the folk medium whenever it is appropriate to her pedagogical or artistic desires.

Interestingly, the government has recognized the educative force of folklore and is currently utilizing it to reinforce certain attitudes about male-female relations as well as the home and the state in the face of what is feared to be a Western sociocultural onslaught. Moroccan television, for example, has serialized the lives of certain folk characters, such as Lalla Fufiya, the simpleminded and ever-erring wife and housekeeper. Beginning with well-known episodes of this popular tale, the medium has added new episodes with similar messages. Significantly, their occurrence on television appears to give such tales a credibility which individual folktellers are not able to generate for themselves with new tales. Television viewers recount the new episodes to nonviewing audiences and in so doing, both have, to a degree, been drawn temporarily back into the realities of a less Westernized sexual world.

THE CORPUS

Thirty-five tales are presented in this volume from a larger corpus of 95 tales that this author collected, compiled, and translated with an eye toward determining Moroccan's beliefs about maleness, femaleness, and sexuality. In all cases, the tales were offered freely and rendered spontaneously by various folktellers, who

used them to educate and/or entertain both this anthropologist
and their Moroccan audiences. Both males and females, aged
approximately 7 to 70, comprise the 14 recounters whose contributions are found in the larger corpus. All are current residents of
the southern Moroccan city of Taroudannt and its environs, and
all heard and learned their tales from oral sources within the
region.

The tales presented here all seem to be of long standing in the
area, even in those cases in which they did not originate within it,
and many have a notably local cast. This thread of local distinc-
tiveness, which has a certain constancy in terms of how male-
female relations are depicted, is apparent in various kinds of tales.
The Moroccan version of Hansel and Gretel (tale 12), which is
one of a number of tales that appear to be of European prove-
nance (Buret 1947), they having reached Morocco a substantial
number of years back, presents boyhood and girlhood quite
differently than does the Grimm version. So, too, does the tale of
the saint Rabi'a al-Adawiyya (tale 19) have its own particular
content: one of a number of religious tales, the Taroudannt tale of
the female saint Rabi'a reconstitutes the saint's life, representing
her as a prostitute rather than the sexually unyielding mystic that
she putatively was (Smith 1928).

It should be emphasized that projections about maleness and
femaleness can come from quite unexpected quarters even in the
Taroudannt folklore. The 95 tales that involve men and women
are an obvious source of such data, but even the animal tales—
tales about the frog, turtle, porcupine, greyhound—sometimes
carry important messages about what maleness and femaleness
are and how male and female are likely to behave. Here one
might mention the association of certain animal species with one
particular sex. The chimpanzee was once an old woman (tale 10),
the crow an old man (tale 29), the frog superordinately female:
particular males and females were believed to be transformed into

these different species as punishments from Allah. In turn, different species are sometimes seen as specifically male or female. In the words of one old woman folkteller, in what remains her own rather than a general folk notion, the frog is the female and the turtle is her husband. The distance between husband and wife emerges as species-large.

The frog-turtle female-male analogy is an interesting spin-off from a conception—that the distance between male and female natures is considerable—that has a more generalized audience among Moroccans. The Taroudannt folklore, I believe, provides an appropriate medium for examining these and other ideas, for folklore, in the end, is essentially societal expression. The Saussurian notion is apt and to the point: "No doubt everything in the folk tale originates with the individual, just as all sound changes must; but this necessary fact of invention ... is somehow the least essential characteristic of folk literature. For the tale does not really become a folk tale, given the oral diffusion of this literature, with its obvious dependence on word of mouth circulation, until the moment when it has been accepted by the listeners who retain it and pass it on. Thus the crucial moment for the folk tale is not that of the *parole,* that of its invention or creation . . . , but that of the *langue;* and we may say that no matter how individualistic may be its origin, it is always anonymous or collective in essence" (Jameson 1972: 29). The ensuing analysis looks at some of these collective phenomena, and attempts, through a consideration of the power relations associated with them, to determine their flesh-and-blood importance for Moroccans and thereby why they are inculcated and retained.

ACKNOWLEDGMENTS

I owe much of my pleasure in planning and writing this volume to friends, family, and colleagues. It was begun after the completion of my doctoral training at Yale and grew and developed during several years of teaching at Columbia, and it evinces the input of both of those institutions. It is also a product of a continuing involvement with Moroccans and a live academic exchange with specialists in the area of Morocco and the Middle East from the time of my first fieldwork. And it is a partial mirror of the development of my own intimate concerns, which friends and family have helped shape during these years.

I owe Yale University's Department of Anthropology my appreciation for a course of training that was far-reaching, thorough, and sensitive. Leopold Pospisil, my doctoral advisor, encouraged my first interest in law, which then grew into a broader interest in social control processes, ideology among them. Harold Conklin and Floyd Lounsbury instilled a deep appreciation for language, and along with Sidney Mintz, Harold Scheffler, Richard Henderson, and others promoted a sense of the crucial importance of good ethnography coupled with good ideas.

I thank the Anthropology Department at Columbia University for providing a fertile environment for the development of anthropological ideas, particularly political ones. Robert Murphy provided support of the finest and most complete sort for the writing of this volume, through the richness of his thinking and the quality of his person. By analyzing Middle Eastern situations in continually new ways, Conrad Arensberg extended a model of what Middle Eastern scholarship can and should be. I owe thanks to Alexander Alland, Bette Denich, Morton Fried, Margaret Mead, Leith Mullings, Elliott Skinner, and other colleagues for their support. The Anthropology Department staff is gratefully acknowledged for its help in the preparation of the manuscript at its various stages.

I first presented some of these ideas at a conference of Moroccanists at Princeton several years ago. Hildred Geeltz the conference's organizer, Clifford Geertz, and others provided insightful comments at that time, as also have other Moroccanists, among them Malcolm Blincow, Paul Rabinow, and Lawrence Rosen. The New York Women's Anthropological Conference provided a second forum for testing these and other ideas, and I wish to thank Constance Sutton, Sue Makiesky, Laura Klein, and the other members for their support. Columbia University's Middle East Institute facilitated this work through a fruitful exchange of ideas.

The role of family and friends in influencing this endeavor and the career that encompasses it is too complex to describe here. Kevin Dwyer lovingly provided a total environment for the growth of these ideas and shared the varied experiences of student life, fieldwork, and career. Shirley Gorenstein extended the care and concern of abiding friendship and the help of a fine intellect. My family by birth and my family through marriage are deeply thanked for their attention, love, and support. The support of friends—Marsha Sieger Bensoussan, Carole Turbin, Anne Forer, and others—is also appreciatively acknowledged.

Finally, I wish to thank my friends and acquaintances in Taroudannt for the opportunity to live and work with them in what will always remain a unique time of my life which I lovingly remember.

Chapter One

INTRODUCTION

Aisha reminisced. She had been born into a life of hardship, her mother having died shortly after her birth. Her father, just and devout, had done the pilgrimage to Mecca in its difficult years and studied religious lore. People agreed that he was to be admired. But soon he married again and his second wife caused him to forget the needs of his child. First Aisha was sent to help in a neighbor's household; then she was given in marriage.

Like many young girls too unsure to voice their protests, Aisha was married to a man from the countryside. And if life in the city had been difficult because of family circumstances, life there proved doubly hard. She had to fetch brush for the fire, run water into the ditches, milk cows, and do other chores. She did these quite well, she recalled, for there had been cows in her father's house and her family had grain holdings which she had helped process in years past. She was by no means a simple city maiden.

And yet her mother-in-law could not be satisfied: she said that the fourteen-year-old was scrawny, haughty, and avoided work in the sun so that she could remain white. The girl had illusions, the old woman would say, which country life simply could not work out of her.

After six months of this unhappiness, Aisha walked out. She gathered her silver and various articles of clothing into an old suitcase while others were busy at work. She still, Aisha says, does not know the number of kilometers that she walked. But distance did not matter. She knew herself to be pregnant in a family that needed more hands. Were her condition to become known, she would be permanently trapped in her husband's household as its childbearer. The moment had come for her return home.

Husband's father called upon her father in an effort to force the bride's return, but despite his requests, Aisha's father remained intractable. With time, the groom's family decided that Aisha's departure spelled no real loss. Her affines asked for a small sum of money in compensation and provided a divorce. Afterward, when Aisha bore a daughter, its father disclaimed the child, calling it "child of a whore." Neighbors shrugged their shoulders at the charges, for they could not know, and yet they also listened eagerly. Some assumed the worst, for that "was the way of women"; others seemed more practical: why care about what a woman does privately if she is publicly proper, appearing on the street, as they would say, "without the man on her back"?

Aisha took in laundry during those first months of divorced life, and remarried later that same year, this time to a tailor who had spotted her in the marketplace. He showed interest, and she reciprocated, eventually accepting his proposal of marriage. But the second marriage also proved hard, this even with the new element of free choice that she earned as a non-virgin. She had expectations about this city man which he in no way fulfilled. He was economically unpredictable, she said, as men were wont to be, and also sexually erring. "I am ashamed to pass by the grocer for I am deeply in debt to him. And yet I must continually buy, this for my children's sake."

After eighteen years, there were six children still living, two children dead, and one fetus miscarried. Her older children had grown up. (Here the reminiscing became hard.) The two eldest sons had dropped out of school. At fifteen and seventeen, neither worked full time nor showed any signs of becoming responsible. Instead they caroused with their peers, smoked, and cruised the streets.

"It is for this reason that I found my oldest son a wife," Aisha said as she pointed to the girl. "I thought she might bring him to his senses, and in any case would help me in the house. I am tired. But she is stubborn and close-mouthed. She eats alone in the kitchen even though we give her a fair share of food. And she tries to tear my son from me, causing trouble between us. She wants him only in the bedchamber, for alas, women want nothing but sex. They are built that way: their minds are in their genitals. But a bride is there to cook, sweep, and launder, not to be liked by her husband. As in all past things, I have again made a poor deal."

To watch Aisha live was to watch a confident, effective woman at work. She overshadowed her husband, who brought home food and money: he sometimes provided, but she proved to be the ongoing manager, juggling money and debts. She channeled her children or attempted to lead them to success and security, over their occasional complaints and her husband's protests: he preferred immediate returns from his children. She was successful with neighbors, who knew that they could count on her aid, in part because she was poor but also because they knew that she would venture alone down important routes. And she won over this anthropologist through her strong sense of self as she maneuvered so well in all these worlds.

Thus the potency of Aisha's opposition to a daughter-in-law perceived as menacing came as no shock. Aisha was nearly ready to do battle at the time of her reminiscing, and was already formulating the defense which would enable her to say that she fought her daughter-in-law with cause. No sense of family; no sense of propriety over food; no realization of the proper place of sex: Aisha could not doubt that anyone would sympathize with her against someone of such unwholesome mentality.

She phrased the issue so that she felt that I, her audience, could not help but understand. In so doing, she called upon what she felt were the indisputables regarding femaleness: the insatiable sexuality of women, their proclivity for causing conflict, the powers that they have and use to destroy the well-being of a man. Hers were descriptions which have the ring of truth for the majority of Moroccans, male and female.

What is striking, of course, is that the speaker was a woman like Aisha. Her own past, as she portrayed it, and, as nearly as I can ascertain, lived it, reveals a woman who had been wrongly accused of precisely the same weaknesses. Her own past reflects the same unhappiness which her daughter-in-law experienced in the new home. And yet Aisha prepared to become the most potent force in subjugating her daughter-in-law. Although she had experienced injustice because she was a woman, she proceeded to single out womanhood as the chief evil to be fought.

The existence of such feelings among women like Aisha, and among those women who are less confident and clever than she, is the focal point of this volume. How does half a population, strong and independent-minded persons among them, come to believe in stereotypes that are self-denigrating? What powers lie behind these formulations that even painfully sustained injustice cannot revise these injurious views? The phenomenon of Aisha raises crucial questions regarding the nature of individual and group consciousness.

It also raises more general questions about the functioning of certain societies that might be called inegalitarian. Most immediately, it leads us to ask how the subordination of certain groups is perpetuated, given the only occasional use of force against many and given the variety of potentially powerful weapons which certain subordinated peoples have at hand. Why do women in Morocco, potential wielders of the power to revise their situations through their control over the socializing of succeeding genera- tions and through the cover that the seclusion of women affords, continue to live in a state of subordination to men? Why do those women leave the image of their inferiority essentially unchal- lenged? A consideration of these questions is relevant not only to an understanding of sexual dynamics in Morocco but also in India, the larger Middle East, Mediterranean Europe, Latin America, and numerous other societies which structure male-female relations in their own particular ways but which might loosely be grouped as sexually inegalitarian. The consideration of the case of sexual inequality also has implications for the understanding of inequality of other kinds (e.g., racial).

In the chapters that follow, I consider why the images of maleness and femaleness that Moroccan men and women hold are persuasive and how these images buttress, and occasionally undermine, existing power relations between men and women. What emerges is an ideational structure that is elaborate and artful. I wish to stress this, for anthropologists have too often done studied peoples an unwitting disservice by focusing upon certain aspects of particular belief systems and then deeming the totality simple or incomplete. The very parsimony of many anthropologi- cal models, which do not sufficiently ground themselves in the intricacies of the encompassing systems, tends to encourage the conclusion that the belief systems studied are uncomplicated and that their adherents thus might be primitive and naïve. One cannot help but feel that thoughtful women in any society should be able to recognize the limitedness of a "woman is to man as nature is to culture" analogy (Ortner 1974) or of a "woman is to man as life-giving is to life-taking" paradigm (Rosaldo 1975), if

culture/nature

these are truly the essential, pivotal points in many sexual ideologies, as some anthropologists assert. Confusion about political realities proceeds from such simplified representations: one suspects that the women involved should be able to counteract the subordination that is validated through such belief systems, and one wonders why they do not.

The analysis that follows takes as given the fact that working ideological systems are complex and highly persuasive. It proceeds from the premise that if millions of women in any sexually inegalitarian society are subordinated, and, indeed, take part in their own subordination, the sexual beliefs that support that condition must be phrased and joined so as to induce believability. It also forwards the parallel premise that if millions of men in those same societies maintain a sense of their own justness and propriety as they take part in inegalitarian exchanges, they do so in part because an imposing network of beliefs imbues many of their actions with an aura of worthwhileness and dignity. From the viewpoint of both male and female participants, the system emerges as artfully constructed. In turn, only through a careful consideration of this artfulness can a full understanding of sexual inequality, as its adherents perceive, espouse, implement, manipulate, and occasionally reject it, be faithfully attained.

Chapter Two
THE PLAY OF PERCEPTIONS:
THE CITY AND ITS FOLK

SETTING

For the most part, the people of the city of Taroudannt, Morocco, still wear their Arab-Barber heritage somewhat unself-consciously. Unlike the inhabitants of cities like Casablanca or Rabat that lie to the north or on the coast, Taroudannt's citizenry has had to contend only minimally with the presence of Europeans. Situated in the southern reaches of a nation that was penetrated primarily from the north, Taroudannt was settled by relatively few French people and experienced French hegemony relatively lightly and late. The French Protectorate in Morocco lasted from 1912 to 1956, for example, but the southern region was not totally subdued until the 1930s. Northern Moroccans witnessed the influx of numerous French colonists who then carved out agricultural domains and established trade networks in that region, while people in the Taroudannt area experienced

7

French contact seldom: there, the French were largely concentrated in military garrisons or in the hospitals, schools, and courts. And if its southerly location has left the city less directly touched even into the present, so, too, has its inland location continued to render it rather impervious to European contact. Nestled eighty kilometers inland in a hot and dry plain, the city tends to this day to be shunned by European tourists and settlers.

Thus the city of Taroudannt displays a less radical dislocation of style, goals, and images from the past than have certain other regions of Morocco. The city has not shifted its economic priorities dramatically in order to avail itself of the lure of international markets, as, for example, have certain of Morocco's larger cities. Nor has it intensively put its Arab-Berber face on view to secure a portion of Morocco's thriving tourist trade. Some farmers within the region have sought a European market for their olives and oranges, and a number of entrepreneurs have worked at attracting what still remains a trickle of tourists; but the preponderant number of Roudaniyin, or Taroudannt dwellers, tend toward an indirect involvement with European paradigms, strategies, knowledge, and affairs.

For Moroccans who call themselves "modern," Taroudannt is frequently adjudged to be a doomed city because of its seemingly introspective, "traditional" stance. It and regions like it occasion their scorn. For most inhabitants of the Taroudannt region, however, the city's image is quite different: Taroudannt continues to be regarded as a busy regional center that attracts attention and people.

The city is rather well located for the maintenance of this internal image of vitality. It is situated in the heart of the Souss Plain, some five kilometers from the Souss River. The plain, in turn, is situated between two mountain ranges, the High Atlas to the north and the Anti-Atlas to the south. Both the plains and the mountains contribute goods and people, much as do the desert regions of the south, for which Taroudannt more occasionally provides camelherders with a refuge. Indeed, fully a third of the city's approximately 15,000 inhabitants are immigrants whom economic interest or necessity has lured from their various locales. In turn, many of those peoples continue to maintain strong ties with their home regions so that the interchange of peoples remains lively and continuing.

While outsiders sometimes see Taroudannt's economy as unprogressive—for example, no factories have been built within the city's walls—both city and region remain productive in terms of the goals of most of their inhabitants. Artisans sell their handicrafts (e.g., sandals, robes, blankets, ironwork, baskets) in the marketplace or in their shops. Traders carry their wares to and from many regions. Farmers tend their gardens, orchards, pastures, and fields inside the city limits and in the outlying area. Their produce is varied. Fruits and vegetables (particularly oranges and olives) and three major grains (wheat, barley, and corn) are the area's chief crops, while sheep, goats, and cows are the main grazing animals. Produce of this kind, which can constitute a varied and healthful diet for Roudaniyin, passes through the city's Thursday and Sunday markets, while manufactured items reach consumers through the city's numerous small stores. Moreover, a considerable number of laborers from both the city and the countryside find work through personalized arrangements or through the *muqef,* or city labor market.

The city of Taroudannt thus has maintained economic importance in its region into the recent period. It has not remained unchallenged, however. The town of Ouled Teima lies halfway between Taroudannt and the coastal city of Agadir. It is located in the heartland of the modern farming sector, while Taroudannt lies on the peripheries. It is open, on either side of the main roadway, unlike Taroudannt, which has an ancient and imposing mud wall encircling it. Its houses and stores are of cement in the modern style, while Taroudannt's are primarily of mud brick. Capital of the neighboring region, Ouled Teima has thrived, its trade level increasing and its political functions proliferating. With regard to those farmers who hold both cities in their purview, there is now an alternative to Taroudannt and so also a degree of competition.

It is most markedly in the realm of politics that Taroudannt has lost power and prestige. Capital of a Shiʻite principality in the eleventh century, base of resistance to the Portuguese five centuries later, stronghold of numerous rulers who intermittently spread their control over the Souss in the preprotectorate days, Taroudannt was long the southern region's political and military heart. That political preeminence has been lost through a revision of national priorities, policies, and goals, and through the redrawing of provincial boundaries. In particular, Taroudannt has lost power and prestige to the more Westernized, coastal city of Agadir. Thus, although Taroudannt remains an administrative center in its own right and is also a regional center for the outlying area, it no longer dominates the larger unit. Instead it has been subsumed into Agadir province, which looks to Agadir city for its political and economic leadership—a leadership that has larger-than-regional concerns. That city is rapidly moving toward fulfilling a Westernized conception of modernity. After its tragic destruction eighteen years ago by an earthquake, it rebuilt itself into a model modernized city. Its hotels line the oceanside; many of its adolescents parade in Western swimsuits on the beach; there is an efflorescence of shopping plazas and a lively tourist trade. Agadir's history has spawned an attentiveness to Western ways as the source of a new identity. Taroudannt, by contrast, responds to its own unique history far from stagnantly, but primarily by keeping its long and convoluted history and heritage at hand. The success of Agadir, like the success of Ouled Teima, has shaken the

confidence of Taroudannt's leadership to a degree, but for Roudaniyin at large, the sum total of developments that comprise the
Agadir pathway are far from wholeheartedly accepted. Those
who are drawn to life of the Agadir sort tend to move out of
Taroudannt to the larger cities; for the most part, there is faith in
the city's life-style among those who remain.

PEOPLE

Residents say that the name *Taroudannt* is Berber in origin. An
aroudan is a pinnacle, while the *t*'s that encompass it signal the
feminine. (Most Berber cities are designated by the feminine.) City
of ramparts, dotted with minarets, Taroudannt is well depicted by
the name, whatever the now-forgotten initial stimulus for it.

There is significance in the fact that the city's name is Berber-
ized. Long-standing residents of the city proudly insist that they
are not Berber but Arab. Some speak only Arabic, which is the
first language of the city, and most say that they practice Arab
manners and customs in their daily lives. But the Arab background tends, in fact, to be temporally shallow for almost all
Roudaniyin, whatever they profess. A close examination of
genealogies reveals some recent Berber ancestry for almost all the
city's inhabitants. It is rare to find a Roudaniy who in no way
shares in the Berber heritage.

The Arab-Berber distinction thus emerges as at once real and
unreal, and otherwise maintains this complexity. It is more cor-
rectly a geographical and linguistic distinction: Berber is the
broader language type that was originally spoken by North
Africa's indigenous population, while Arabic is the language of the
Muslim conquerors from the east. Berber continued to be spoken
predominantly in the less easily conquered mountain regions and

in parts of the plain, while Arabic infiltrated mainly the plains and the cities. But even the linguistic and topological dichotomies are ambiguous, as the Taroudannt case itself suggests. Although the two languages are, in essence, mutually incomprehensible, Taroudannt Arabic contains numerous Berber words, and the city's Berber has its marked Arabic element. Similarly, exclusively Berber-speaking or Arabic-speaking Roudaniyin do not constitute the city's population. Berbers tend to learn Arabic upon their entry into the city, the men and children first and then the women, while many city-born residents also develop an acquaintance with some Berber for economic and social reasons. In terms of linguistic involvement, the city scarcely houses two well-defined groups.

If a dichotomy between Berbers and Arabs is far from accurate in terms of what people speak, a Berber-Arab distinction is even less appropriate in terms of cultural elements. Predominantly Berber and Arabic speakers tend to live and behave similarly. They are all Muslims and hold comparable values, norms, and beliefs. Indeed, they are often indistinguishable in dress, manner, and physique.

And yet there is the matter of stereotypes and images. Taroudannt's "Arabs" evince a certain pride in their "Arab" identity and in large part validate their positive sense of self by elaborating upon their contrast with the "Berber" outsiders. The "Arab" city dwellers see themselves as sophisticated: they claim that they have a penchant for high living, while the "Berbers" are said to be primitive in their behavior and tastes. "Berbers," they say, eat nothing but lentils, cook their chickens insufficiently, and are stingy, largely because of their inadequate awareness of how money is best spent. A touch of the noble savage also colors the image: "Berbers" are portrayed as family-centered and religious, while the "Arab" city dwellers are wont to admit that they exhibit hedonistic motivations.

The contrast with the "Berbers" provides the Taroudannt population with a continuing sense of self-worth in these changing times, a feeling which seems to have been previously sustained in part through comparison with the city's Jewish population. Those Jews, who numbered approximately 1,000 in 1948 (Morales 1948: 66), lived within their own city quarter, spoke their own dialect, and worked at what Muslims saw as particularly Jewish jobs (e.g., tailoring, lantern manufacture, sieve making). The Jews' image among the local Muslims was strongly negative. They were said to be sloppy and dirty; they were described as sexually wanton, marrying their uncles and aunts; even their *jnun,* humans' spiritual parallels in the netherworld, were described as especially difficult and irascible. Burdened with this stereotype and interacting from a continuing position of weakness, the vast majority of Jews emigrated to France or Israel. Less than twenty now remain.

The Taroudannt "Arab," then, has had his cultural identity challenged only gently from various spheres while still maintaining his recourse to long-standing sources of self-validation. Mountain Berbers continue to flow into the city: the influx reaffirms the city's image of superiority for the city's residents. The Taroudannt Jewish community is no longer found, but occasionally its memory still provides grounds for reaffirming an "Arab-Muslim" Roudaniy ideal. The presence of the French had its impact, but it was and still is largely indirect. The French first entered Taroudannt in 1917, but at that time and afterward, most French residents lived apart. This is still true for the French who work in the city's hospitals and schools: they group together and interact only cursorily with the city's residents. Shielded from day-to-day contact with them, Roudaniyin tend to adopt a French perspective only occasionally in evaluating their own lives and indeed compare their own lives with those of the French quite infrequently.

Comparison more often is made with the amalgam of European and Middle Eastern life-styles that the inhabitants of Casablanca, Agadir, and other large Moroccan cities present. But these cities are also viewed as displaying a certain decadence in conjunction with the dynamism that spells success in the wider world. Given this continuing negative face of the image, the challenge that these cities pose to the more familiar life-style of Taroudannt dwellers can still be contained and absorbed, at least at this time.

THE SEPARATION OF THE SEXES

One sphere in which Taroudannt residents encounter aspects of the so-called modern way of life concerns male-female relations. "Modern" modes of presentation, and more limitedly "modern" modes of interaction, occasionally make their way into Taroudannt from the larger cities, and the Roudaniy response tends to be cautious, selective, and often rejecting. Female children wear Western clothing—sweaters and pants—before puberty, for example, but almost no proper woman wears such dress after reaching adulthood. Instead women shift to the veil and 'izar (a black, white, or blue sheet that totally encompasses the wearer) or djellaba (a flowing, full-length robe that is taken as a sign of prestige). Brides sometimes wear makeup when they debut during the wedding week (brides used to apply native eye darkener and rouge at these times), but women, married or not, must not use makeup in everyday life. By extension, some boys and girls meet cursorily in back alleys—the number of these secret rendez-vous, in fact, is increasing and forms a prelude to marriage in some cases—but boys and girls virtually never walk or talk together publicly, as is the French style. The Taroudannt woman or girl who violates these strictures endangers her reputation. She is not merely mimicking the European woman but is also approximating the mien of the Moroccan street prostitute—made up, boldly smoking a cigarette, occasionally wearing Western garb, and familiarly approaching whatever males happen to pass by. The reputable woman must avoid the association.

Instead the tendency for both sexes is toward a quite different, well-trodden path: the separation of the sexes in everyday life. Taroudannt women spend the bulk of their time with girls and other women, while men spend most of their time with other males. Interaction between the sexes, when it occurs, is generally restricted and regulated.

Separation between the sexes continues to be evident in most aspects of Taroudannt life. It is immediately apparent, for example, when the two sexes maneuver in public. In the streets, women walk alone or in the company of children and other women, while men walk alone or in the company of men. This is true for married couples as well as single persons and is also true when husbands and wives go out in tandem. Some husbands walk a block or so behind their wives on such occasions so that they can watch their spouses' every action while preventing onlookers from mentally associating them with their women. In these and other cases, both sexes opt for modesty, with men additionally showing an institutionalized distrust. *examples*

The separation of men and women extends into virtually all aspects of public life. Cafés are frequented only by men: women cannot enter them. Stores are serviced almost exclusively by males. The few women who work in shops do so because their stores are sheltered and their menfolk are absent. Even then, those women tend to rest in the backs of their shops in the shadow until a familiar customer comes by. In another vein, governmental policy reinforces the principle of male-female separation on festive occasions. At a 1970 celebration held in honor of King Hassan, male and female observers were placed in separate groups in the city plaza to observe the singing and dancing. They were separated by barriers, with police guarding the lines.

The separation of men from women is also apparent in more private settings. At celebrations that are held for friends and family, women congregate separately from those men who are guests. On these occasions, each sex has its own entertainers, who are almost always of the same sex as their audience. Men might invite *fuqara,* religious devotees who recite the Koran from memory; women might hire *shexat,* women who sing praises of guests while the guests dance along. The one major exception to the practice of same-sexed entertainment lies in the male sphere: men sometimes hire dancing prostitutes to entertain them.

The division between male and female groups extends to the less rigidly defined moments of everyday socializing. Women tend to gather with women friends and neighbors in the home or more occasionally in the public bath during the daytime women's hours. So satisfying is the bath experience from the point of view of female companionship that women tend to stay in the bath for long stretches of time, as men often lament. They bring oranges for refreshment and also bring their children, so that there will be no worries or interruptions. Then they stay, sometimes scrubbing themselves but more often just lazing in the hot steaming environment as they listen to gossip. Men, by contrast, do not need to remain in the bath for long hours, for they have other occasions on which to interact with their male friends in a leisurely fashion. They meet in stores, gardens, and cafés for long hours, since male company is deemed pleasurable while men tend to regard women's company as unfulfilling and burdensome.

The separation of the sexes is maintained most consistently and is explained most explicitly within the realm of religion. Islam is male in its most public, most formal organizational aspects. Men pray in the mosques, make up the membership rolls of the religious brotherhoods, and are the religious leaders of the community of Islam. Virtually all Taroudannt saints, for example, are male. The women of Taroudannt are generally excluded from these roles and from the more visible devotions. Taroudannt women are prohibited from praying in the main Muslim worship areas that are located in the mosques; it is said that if they should menstruate there, the mosque and all those within it would fall into a state of pollution. Their devotions are limited to the home or to those very few sparse cubicles which are reserved for women in a limited number of mosques. Women utilize even these infrequently, all but a few older women realizing that a woman best protects her modesty and reputation by praying at home.

The religious brotherhoods, powerful Muslim organizations, in almost all instances limit their membership to men and do not permit women to enter their lodges. Those few groups that do permit women's participation insist that women form separate groups, each with its own meeting place, functions, and hierarchy of officials (Dwyer 1978). Such separation is believed to be sanctioned by Allah for the purpose of succoring religious zeal by limiting sexual temptation and involvement.

In the economic realm, the sexes are segregated, Roudaniyin affirm, for a similar purpose: to maintain the purity of women and thereby also their families' honor. As a result of these considerations, Taroudannt residents say, few occupations can be performed by both men and women, and women's and men's work areas need to be discretely defined. Women who need or want to supplement their families' incomes, for example, work at such jobs as curing, midwifery, wool spinning, sewing, cooking, and laundering, tasks which are part-time and generally undertaken in the household, while men tend to engage in artisanry, trading, selling—nonhousehold jobs. In most cases, women constitute women's main clients, and in almost all cases, male-female inter-

cutoff

actions within the economic sphere are truncated, being shorter
and less personalized than those which occur between members
of the same sex.

In like manner, marketplace activities in Taroudannt are predominantly male, with men constituting the main producers,
transporters, and distributors of goods. Men sell livestock, meat,
vegetables, clothing, and housewares, these being arranged in
separate sections of the marketplace. The relatively few women
who sell handle only certain kinds of produce, such as eggs,
poultry, bread, and ready-to-eat items. Women prepare these
foods or raise their animals in their homes and then sell them
within discrete areas of the marketplace (*suq*).

There is a similar physical separation between men and women
who work on the area's many farms. Both sexes can be hired as
farm workers, but the separation of the sexes is generally marked.
During an olive harvest, men shake the olives from the branches
while rows of women gather up the fruit. During a wheat or barley
harvest, men cut the grain and then gather the stalks, often
accompanied by women, who are paid lower wages and who
work in rows that are located farther off. Conflict is expected if
men and women are mixed.

The principle of male-female separation affects the ground plan
for city politics much as it does economic behavior. The visitor to
the office of the *qaid,* the region's highest political official, discovers women waiting outside, in separate areas from men. The
observer in the Taroudannt court finds two locations for litigants,
one male and one female. Male litigants sit in the courtroom
awaiting their cases while female litigants are kept outside by the
court police: women sit on the steps of the court building or in a
nearby garden. It is only when their cases are immediately being
considered that they are permitted to enter the courtroom. Then,
when a woman appears before the judge, formality and reserve
characterize the interaction. Women generally exhibit reticence

and modesty in the courtroom setting, and male officials feel that it is decorous to solicit women's testimony and opinions less intensively. When possible, male witnesses and male representatives are questioned in women's stead. As a result, political or judicial interactions involving women remain formal and terse, a tendency which works to women's disadvantage.

The geographical map of the legal and political domains mirrors the division of labor within them. Men fill the political offices within the region; they staff the regular and court police, and work as judge, notary, and scribe in the Taroudannt court system. Indeed, only one female official is attached to the Taroudannt political system or judiciary: the *'arifa* or "woman who knows." Appointed by the courts and paid for her services by interested parties, the *'arifa* collects information from women for the courts. She protects women when the police forcibly enter homes, she detains those women whom husbands designate as rebellious, and she checks a woman's virginity and pregnancy when these are disputed. Because male officials are prohibited from entering into such exchanges with female outsiders, the *'arifa* emerges as an essential liaison between the sexes (Dwyer 1977).

Despite the marked divisions between the sexes, it can, of course, in no way be said that Taroudannt's men and women lead mutually exclusive lives. Apart from their sexual involvements, spouses traditionally take their meals together, unless guests are present. In most families, they provide advice to one another and frequently exchange gossip. Many Moroccan wives are hard-driving, assertive women, and many more are quietly persuasive and unyielding. Through one means or another, they make their voices heard and attempt to influence male-run affairs.

Similarly, men project themselves into predominantly female concerns, with fathers and brothers, particularly, showing concern and interest in their daughters' and sisters' futures and welfare. A father, for example, makes the final decision regarding a daughter's marriage, while a brother tends to become his sister's primary moral guardian, for he has access to the detailed and often delicate information that is provided by his peer group. As a consequence, he quickly learns about any indiscretions involving his sister and generally chastises her should embarrassments arise. The relationships of brothers and sisters, like those of fathers and daughters, are often conflict ridden through the real or threatened application of constraints and punishments, although they also tend to evince a positive component of concern and affection.

Outside the family, intimacy between male and female occurs predominantly in the context of illicit sexual relations. Whereas a spouse is expected to engage in sexual relations in order to conceive children for the family, a lover provides sex for physical gratification, and perhaps for passion and love, and, from the standpoint of many women, for the material benefits that the giving of sexual favors provides. Because these relationships are sometimes an occasion for a convoluted and elaborate sexuality and because they are often characterized by an easy familiarity, they often fulfill important needs that marriage cannot.

Whatever the physiological and psychological benefits to both parties, women who provide or receive sexual favors outside marriage are technically prostitutes by law. They can be arrested and imprisoned should outsiders notify the police: the home of any Taroudannt woman, for example, can be raided by the police when accompanied by the *'arifa* if that woman is entertaining a man illicitly. This threat holds for ostensibly proper women much as for the city's contingent of prostitutes, who distinguish themselves, it is felt, not so much through their lesser moral nature but rather by their flamboyant demeanor and appearance as they parade in the city's more notorious streets.

The ethic of sexual modesty that separates most men from women begins to be inculcated in children's early years. Already at the age of three or four, boys are found together, playing with other neighborhood boys in the street. Typically, girls do not join them. They are more closely restricted to the home area and are quickly drawn into female concerns. Girls begin housework at the age of five or six, when they help to clean the house and care for younger siblings. By the age of twelve or thirteen, they are expected to display a womanlike proficiency at all household chores. At that age, contrary to law but in accordance with custom, they are ready to wed.

The introduction of French elements into the Taroudannt school system has broken down the rigidity of these patterns to a degree. Boys and girls now attend the same lycée, although the two sexes still remain apart in the lower grades. And although parents still enjoy the option of keeping their daughters out of school, those young girls who do attend perforce are propelled into a more public world. Some degree of male-female interaction inevitably occurs on the streets and in the schools. It should be noted, however, that parents are always aware of the possibility of scandal that this heightened exposure affords, and often respond defensively. Partly because of their fears, parents tend to withdraw their daughters from classes when those girls near puberty, if not before, thereafter keeping them tied to the home whatever their academic capabilities.

However much sexual modesty is expected in women's behavior, individual variability, as always, exists. One woman might flee from a room when confronted with her husband's male guests, while another might greet those men and then continue to remain apart in the same room. An outgoing woman might consult a male doctor about her physical ailments, while one who is more modest might find herself unable to seek male medical help. Similarly, one husband might allow his wife to shop in the marketplace, while another might deny her such access, he going to the shops personally to bring home a selection of clothing and food.

In comparison to Moroccans in some other regions, Taroudannt's inhabitants have demonstrated a considerable tenacity in their adherence to these patterns of sex segregation. This phenomenon might well be associated with community size in addition to regional history. In effect, Taroudannt's size is sufficient to provide men and women with a degree of anonymity which creates an occasion for illicitness, while also assuring a degree of familiarity which can make the community at large easily cognizant of even the most intimate details of a man or woman's life. Thus there is temptation, distrust, and the ever-present possibility of scandal, and also a passionate concern with the maintenance of proper sexual images of self.

MALE DOMINANCE AND FEMALE SUBORDINATION

Sex segregation, of course, does not necessarily imply the subordination of women, nor, indeed, must it imply the subordination of either sex. There is always the theoretical possibility of separate but equal existences. In the Moroccan setting, however, the separation of the sexes is part of a male-female relational system in which women are markedly subordinate. Women have less power, are accorded less authority, and are burdened with legal and extra-legal restrictions which sharply curtail even the most vital of life options.

If domination is a constricting of life alternatives for one group by another group, then women in Morocco constitute the dominated sex. They are severely limited in their ability to change the quality and form of their lives, much more so than men. As table 2.1 demonstrates, the limitations are far-reaching: among other things, restrictions affect the use of one's body, control over offspring, choice of companionship, the option of working, and possibilities for free movement and protest.

The imbalance between male and female options is marked with regard to the 32 rights and privileges listed in table 2.1. Men

Table 2.1: Rights and Privileges

Marriage and Divorce	Women	Men
1) First marriage	She technically must provide her own consent, but her male matrimonial tutor must also approve and represent her	He must consent, but a representative is needed only in the preadult period
2) Polygamy	Prohibited	A man can take up to four wives simultaneously, unless he waives this right in a marriage contract
3) Divorce	Legally acceptable reasons are few (e.g., the husband's prolonged desertion); substantial danger or injustice must be shown	According to the husband's desire
4) Remarriage	Prohibited during the *'idda* period (variably three to nine months after widowhood or divorce)	Immediate remarriage is possible
5) Virginity	Virginity must be proved for the first marriage; the bride-wealth can be halved and the groom has cause to abandon his bride if she is not a virgin	His past sexual experience constitutes no liability
6) Conjugal sex	A wife has the right to sexual attention but no right to withhold sex, except when menstruating	He has a right to sexual attention but can more easily withhold sex, for men's sexual capability is believed to be less
7) Extramarital sex	Prohibited by law; and the violator can be prosecuted for prostitution	Prohibited, but the violator is generally not prosecuted
Parenthood		
8) Guardianship	The divorced wife has prior rights when the child is small, but she must not remarry	Legal guardianship over postpubescent children is legally his rather than the mother's, but often the mother continues her care; no penalties are

(Table 2.1: cont.)

	Women	*Men*
		applied upon his remarriage
9) Legal representation of children (including management of property)	A female representative is possible but rare	Generally the child is provided with a male representative
10) Abortion	A sin and a crime	A sin and a crime if he aids in it
Mobility		
11) Curfew	From sunset to sunrise for all women	From sunset to sunrise but only for youths and nonresidents
12) Seclusion	Tacit or explicit approval of the household head is required for a woman to leave home	No limitations
13) Choice of residence	Women have no say, unless their marriage contracts stipulate	Male household head selects the home
14) Religious attendance	Women are limited to a small number of women's prayer rooms in the city's mosques	All mosques are open to men
Modesty		
15) Contact	Avoidance of eye contact is appropriate with strangers; physical contact should be avoided	Men may look but not touch
16) Dress	Ideally all but the eyes and fingertips should be covered; veiling is generally practiced	Face and lower arms are open to view; there is no veiling
Religious Participation		
17) Devotions (e.g., fasting, touching the Koran, praying)	Prohibitions are operative during menstruation, forty days postpartum, and after intercourse and elimination until ritual washing is completed	Prohibitions are operative after intercourse and elimination until ritual washing is completed
18) Health care	A husband and father is obligated to provide it, but a	As he desires

(Table 2.1: cont.)

	Women	Men
	woman requires male approval for consultations and fee payment	
Communality		
19) Hosting	Minimally, men must give their tacit consent, sometimes even for female visitors	His guests can enter if he is present
20) Visiting family and friends	Traditionally a bride would not visit her family until the completion of one year of marriage; visits to friends can be prohibited by a father or husband; moderate visiting to kinfolk cannot	As he desires
21) Access by parents	Access is legally guaranteed to the woman's parents, but it can be curtailed if excessive and conflict-provoking	As he and they desire
Economics		
22) Work	A widow or divorcee has the privilege of choosing salaried work; the consent of a husband or father is required for other females	As he desires or is necessary for family support
23) Leisure	A wife must do household tasks but can refuse to do salaried labor	Even total leisure is acceptable if his family is supported
24) Inheritance	A woman is generally allocated half the equivalent male's share and this often is forfeited	A male is generally allocated twice the equivalent female's share; no forfeiture occurs
25) Control of salary	Personal control is legally guaranteed, and women often fight to maintain this right; men, however, sometimes seize women's salaries	He has personal control over his own earnings, but must support his family; this includes child support after divorce
26) Purchase	Women now shop to a	As he desires

(Table 2.1: cont.)

	Women	Men
	degree, but their purchases are generally supervised; in a few families they are prohibited from shopping, and this is acceptable by law	
27) Control over property gained in marriage	Bedding, women's clothing, jewelry, and kitchen utensils are presumed to be the woman's	All else is taken to be the husband's, unless the wife can prove otherwise
Judicial Process		
28) Legal representation	Women are often represented by men; male representation is sometimes required (e.g., at a virgin's marriage)	Self-representation suffices
29) Witness	A woman's witness counts half that of a man and is generally not elicited	A man's witness counts twice a woman's and is sought
30) Court attendance	Women are generally excluded from the courtroom	Men can attend those sessions in which their cases occur
Political Involvement		
31) Office holding	A woman cannot be judge, prayer leader, or sultan; this prohibition is informally extended to all political offices	Offices are male-controlled and male-staffed
32) Voting	Adult women can vote, but modesty often prevents women's vote from being cast	Adult men vote and cast their ballots

clearly enjoy greater freedoms in virtually all cases. The two striking exceptions concern guardianship of children and child support. Moroccan courts generally look to women in their search for caretakers for children, and adult males must continue to provide their children with financial support after divorce. But as is also apparent from the table, encumbrances upon women extend even into the guardianship and child support spheres: divorced men often neglect their support payments, while most women, for reasons of modesty, find it difficult to sue for reimbursement; women's guardianship right is also provisional: unlike men, they forfeit that right should they remarry.

The power of men over women is best illustrated in the making and breaking of marriages. On the occasion of a woman's first marriage, she has little input into the decision-making process. It is her father who is approached by suitors, who argues about the money and goods that the groom's family will contribute, and who determines if and when his daughter is to be wed. It is he who validates the wedding contract in the presence of the court's scribes. At most, a potential bride can plead with her father or can seek to influence him through her mother, but she cannot actually accept or reject her suitor. Acceptance requires the father's approval, for he is her legal spokesman. Correspondingly, her father can circumvent even her rightful protests through various means. Thus although a bride technically must consent to her marriage in the presence of court scribes in order for it to be valid, another girl, veiled and so indistinguishable from her, might be presented in her stead. The scribes assume that the girl is the bride-to-be and record her acceptance.

The already once-married woman sustains fewer restrictions as she seeks a spouse, but typically still cannot exercise her free will completely. No longer a virgin, she requires no male spokesman and so can act as her own representative. Considerable variability exists, however, in the extent to which women implement this legal right. More often than not living with her family of origin after widowhood or divorce, a once-married potential bride sinks into a state of semidependence, and tends again to fall under her family's decision-making power.

For the previously married woman, then, legal restrictions lessen, but social and economic pressures continue to limit the open pursuit of new life alternatives. This freedom is further circumscribed by the nature of the public face that a proper woman must show. In no case should a woman appear to be too desirous to wed, for example, for others will interpret her enthusiasm as uncontrolled sexual passion. A man, by contrast, can search out a wife openly at any age. Both men and women validate his search, for he is felt to have greater than sexual goals: he is believed to need someone to care for his home, launder, and cook.

Underlying much of the power that a husband has over his wife is the husband's almost exclusive ability to divorce. Men obtain divorces easily; they merely petition the court. Women cannot sue for divorce directly. Instead each woman must individually convince the judge of the merits of her case. Then, if the judge is won over, he còmmands the husband to divorce the wife that he has offended. It should be noted, however, that judges tend to sympathize with male defendants so that women are at a severe disadvantage during these proceedings. As a consequence, the outcomes are almost inevitable: cases are extended and costly, and few women earn divorces.

Because of women's lesser legal privileges and because of the biases of judges and scribes, women typically do not initiate divorce actions when they seek to terminate their marriages. Instead abandonment becomes the favored recourse. When the husband is absent, at work, or with friends, the wife deserts and domiciles herself with her kinsmen, who assume a protective role toward her. If the wife remains adamant about not returning, the husband eventually sues for divorce. Unfortunately for women, however, this process is not without its pitfalls and penalties. In all desertion cases, the wife forfeits her right to the monetary compensation (ṣḍaq) due to her in the event of divorce. Moreover, the husband still can sue for his wife's return through the courts: a wife who cannot prove just cause for her desertion can be sequestered in the charge of the 'arifa until she shows a change of heart.

(It is felt that women sometimes need such incentives in order to bring them to their senses.) Finally, when a wife deserts him, a husband is in no way compelled to release her. As a consequence, she might be forced to live out her life in a marital limbo: her husband no longer need support her, and yet she is not free to take a new spouse, for she is still technically married. Her husband, by contrast, is legally less constrained, for he can marry as many as three additional women. Faced with these perils, some women take a surer but more costly route: they pay their husbands to divorce them, frequently quite substantially.

The life pathways of Taroudannt women, in many respects tend to be hard. Ironically, the discrepancy between women's and men's life options increases rather than decreases as a family's standard of living increases. Wealthy husbands prefer and can more easily afford to seclude their women, and the wives of wealthy men (apart from the few educated women in the city) prefer not to work for reasons of self-image. These women live in a valued state of social and economic dependence. By contrast, the poor woman must shop, work, and leave her home daily in order to provide for her family's sustenance. Outsiders find her situation unfortunate but inescapable and so are indulgent toward the poor woman's forced freedom as long as her freer behavior is limited to socially necessary tasks. Many working women, however, cautiously overstep these bounds. Many also find that their participation in the labor market gives them greater leverage socially and economically vis-à-vis their husbands.

These restrictions and these attitudes reflect Moroccans' recurrent fears about what are believed to be women's failings. Women cannot administer property dispassionately, it is said, and so they should remain economically dependent upon men. Women are felt to change their evidence in court according to their loves and hatreds, and so only half a "witness" is accorded to them. Women cannot be trusted in the passion-provoking nighttime, and so a curfew is imposed. Women should be modest, shame-faced, and patient; and yet both sexes fear that they cannot be. Subordination is validated for them by that lingering doubt.

MEN'S AND WOMEN'S WORLDS

Kept separate and subordinate, albeit to varying degrees, Tarou-dannt women have tended to develop a woman's world within limited boundaries, a world which is relatively insulated from men. And men, for their part, have developed a man's world into which women only infrequently enter. These worlds do not encompass men's and women's existences, for the two sexes obviously share much common ground. Rather they exist as forced outgrowths of sex segregation while also serving as strategically defined spheres which present a refuge for both sexes from the tensions of male-female relations.

This complex separation and joining of men's and women's worlds reveals itself in the physical and temporal division of life space. The household, for example, is a joint living unit for men and women, but during certain hours it more nearly becomes a female domain. So, too, is the *derb,* or street neighborhood, often a single-sexed locality. Because of restrictions upon women's mobility, women tend to be closely confined to these units, and because men feel that women's company is degrading, men frequently feel compelled to establish themselves outside of them. What results is numerous rather discrete social worlds which appear and disappear at various times.

Family and Household

Taroudannt families (table 2.2) are of various kinds. Most often they are nuclear. Frequently, however, the husband's parents or

Table 2.2: Household Composition in Two Sample Areas

Type of Household	Area 1	Area 2	Total
Nuclear	14 (67%)	25 (58%)	39 (61%)
Simple	9 (43%)	20 (47%)	29 (45%)
With servant	2 (10%)	3 (7%)	5 (8%)
Polygynous separate	1 (5%)	0 (0%)	1 (2%)
With returned married daughter	2 (10%)	2 (5%)	4 (6%)
Extended patrilocal	4 (19%)	6 (14%)	10 (16%)
Extended matrilocal	0 (0%)	2 (5%)	2 (3%)
Fraternal joint	0 (0%)	1 (2%)	1 (2%)
Bachelor female	3 (14%)	3 (7%)	6 (9%)
Bachelor male	0 (0%)	4 (9%)	4 (6%)
Other (kin-based)	0 (0%)	2 (5%)	2 (3%)
	21	43	64

parent is present in what then comprises the traditional ideal extended family form. More rarely, a couple lives with the woman's parents, particularly when the husband is a recent immigrant or the wife's family is rich. Fraternal joint households, in which male siblings live together without their parents but with their wives and children, also occur, as do households that bring together diverse kin. Indeed, whatever ideals are verbalized, considerable variability occurs, a variability that reflects ultimate male decision-making but that is also tied to the desires and behavior of women and men's interpretation of them.

Virtually all Taroudannt marriages are monogamous, this despite the fact that most Moroccans marry a number of times in a lifetime and that polygyny is legally protected. Men say that they avoid the polygynous condition because it requires money and causes problems among their women. Women almost unanimously agree, saying that they will not tolerate co-wives. Almost all men scrupulously heed these warnings: in the rare case that a man has them, co-wives are almost always separately housed.

Whatever its composition, a household is unified (or divided) largely through the actions of its women, or so it is said. Its women tend to spend long hours together: the hours of the curfew and most of the daytime. They eat together, chat together, and work together, generally dividing up jobs so that the older women do the prestige tasks while women of a similar lower status take turns at less valued chores. Women also share household produce and utensils, an arrangement which integrates schedules but which can also lead to bickering. In intimate and continuing contact, such women interact with deep loyalty and affection in some households, with tenseness in others, but generally with strong emotional involvement and minimal reserve.

The males of a household tend to be less intimately tied, making the household much less a male than a female domain. Whether young boy, adolescent, or adult, each leaves his home for many of the daylight hours, to work or to spend his leisure time with other males. Even when at home and together, the men of a household tend to interact with modesty. There is often tension regarding the allocation of authority: this causes cautiousness. There also appears to be an underlying emotional tension, for fathers and sons sometimes have strong and competing emotions vis-à-vis the mother-wife. And as is logical under these circumstances, there is verbal restraint and also a marked bodily modesty: a man and his son or son-in-law do not attend the public bath together, for example, for each experiences shame at the sight of the other's nudity and in the latter case sometimes also a foreboding regarding personal health.

If a household is said to unite largely through the interrelation of its women, a household is said to undergo fission largely because of conflict among women. Daughters-in-law vie with their mothers-in-law over the control of the financial and emotional resources of their men; daughters-in-law vie with each other as to who proves most valuable with respect to housekeeping, fertility, and physical attractiveness. There are numerous occasions for conflict, a reality which leads Moroccans to portray women's household relations quite negatively. Moroccan aphorisms are to the point on these matters: "the sister-in-law is rotten," "the husband's wife is like a louse," "brothers' wives descended from the heavens fighting." To this might be added the fact that the term for mother-in-law (*'aguz*) is also the more general term for a crone.

And yet Moroccans' focus upon the real possibility of female tension also carries its illusion, for male tensions (e.g., the conflict of fathers and sons vying for household control, the tension of brothers sharing a patrimony) tend to be minimized in people's eyes because of it. Moreover, the image of female contentiousness tends to preclude the recognition of the stable and positive aspects of female relationships in many men's and women's minds. The most striking instance of this obfuscation concerns the mother-daughter relationship. Mothers typically intercede on their daughters' behalf during marriage negotiations. When daughters flee from their husbands, mothers most actively support and shelter them against the onslaught of irate husbands. They also tend to extend financial aid in times of crisis and provide ongoing advice. On occasion, they aid their daughters in working through their romances. Moreover, this outpouring of aid and affection is reciprocal: daughters tend to help their mothers in times of need, most Roudaniyin say, more so than sons.

By virtue of a strongly positive mother-daughter tie and through the forced intimacy and occasional affection of its other women, the women of most households are able to act somewhat strategically vis-à-vis their men. Some exchange sorcery secrets so as better to control their husbands. Many provide one another with solace when conjugal life is hard. Others help hide one another's sexual and financial indiscretions. Indeed, the potential for tension that exists in nonnuclear households partially reflects the intimacy and convolutedness of the relationships that more generally characterize women's family life. In this respect even smooth-flowing relationships, like the mother-daughter one, tend to take on a negative "female" cast: they often come to be regarded as divisive and tension-causing to male-female relations.

The Street Neighborhood

The street neighborhood provides a second, highly complex interactional world for women. While certain male activities are carried out within its boundaries, female activities form the primary basis of its social life. Women undertake a variety of tasks within the street: social, religious, political, and economic. Their social networks within it tend to be elaborate. Concurrently, with regard to privileges and obligations, the role of neighbor is much more convoluted for women than for men.

The physical form of most street neighborhoods contributes to the proliferation of contacts and activities among women. By and large, neighborhood streets are culs-de-sac, a form which provides a congenial environment given women's seclusion. Strangers do not enter into local neighborhoods, for they are unable to pass through them to more distant regions. Nonresident shoppers have little cause to frequent them, for few stores exist inside. Nor does curiosity drive visitors into a neighborhood's environs: the lushness or sparseness of homes, fields, and gardens is obscured by the simple mud walls with which street passageways are lined.

Because the street does not draw the attention of outsiders, male or female, women's behavior is freed markedly within it. During the hours that men are at work, women move about rather informally: they go from house to house and from woman friend to woman friend with comparative ease. Most go unveiled; many drape only a towel or sheet over their bodies; some altogether forego wearing their enveloping sheets. In some streets women even gather in unsheltered passageways to work or to gossip.

Friendships between Moroccan women generally arise within these neighborhood units, for its is chiefly there that women can interact in an intense and ongoing manner. Friendship, in the Moroccan sense of the term, necessitates an exchange of gifts and visits, the giving of aid on ceremonial occasions, the open possibility of lending and borrowing, and frequent opportunities for chatting and gossip. Proximity facilitates this behavior, while distance, such as is occasioned by a move out of the neighborhood, often causes even strong friendships to lapse.

The street neighborhood is a multifunctional female unit. It has religious functions which women zealously carry through: at the tombs that are found within a street's boundaries, women typically hold yearly feasts in honor of neighborhood saints. The women of a street also unite on certain social occasions: they take a bride to the public bath on the day of her wedding and are typically invited to any and all family celebrations within the locale. And in a more covert vein, women neighbors often handle goods pilfered from husbands and provide excuses for women who are absent from home because of romantic involvements.

The men of a street neighborhood do not develop comparable social networks. They meet with their neighbors on occasion, but they typically do not involve themselves in local affairs and festivities. Male neighbors, for example, do not help with the preparations for the feasts for street saints, and do not attend the ensuing celebrations. Nor do they invite a substantial percentage of male neighbors to family affairs. Nor again do they typically look to their male neighbors as confidants and compatriots. Instead there is a relative lack of social involvement which tends to reflect the level of male neighbors' feelings about one another: there is some friendliness but also a reserve that reflects broader life options.

Beyond the Neighborhood

Whereas women most often maneuver in the household or the street neighborhood, men generally range more widely as they establish and maintain social ties. They share their interactional world with near and far kinsmen, co-workers, and friends, and do this in diverse localities. Boys and those older men whom Moroccans call irresponsible tend to frequent the cafés. There, they drink tea and coffee, watch television, play checkers, and gossip. Men who are older and of a more religious persuasion avoid these popular haunts and might meet at brotherhood lodges. There, socializing occurs in the context of religious devotions, and members often establish important economic and political ties.

For all men, however, whatever their social or religious inclinations, the workplace, the garden, and the salon, when appropriately insulated from women, provide primary settings for socializing and rest. Friends and kinsmen congregate at storefronts, where they gossip and drink tea. Friends and relatives also meet in privately owned gardens and fields: men sometimes prepare their dinner or supper there or in the workplace in an atmosphere of communality and friendship. On other occasions, men repair to their houses in order to entertain others. Women serve these males, handing them food through scarcely opened doorways, otherwise remaining unseen and apart.

Many women, however, are involving themselves increasingly in arenas beyond the household and neighborhood. The marketplace, the city's shopping areas, and the hospital, for example, now draw Taroudannt women more frequently, as they undertake household and family tasks. In turn, this greater mobility is cited by certain women as the reason for the slow decline in household and neighborhood corporateness. Present-day women, these women say, are blatant in their desire to control goods and services exclusively: hence extended families, which entail a complex division of labor, fall apart more quickly. Involved in more far-ranging activities, "modern" women, they say, neglect extrafamilial activities that occur close to home. Wedding preparations in the neighborhood were once protracted, lasting two weeks or so; now a bride's female neighbors offer their aid at most one or two days before the week of festivities. Children's attainments, like the reaching of the fortieth day or the emergence of teeth, were once locally celebrated; some of these rituals have now been forgotten or take place only among friends or family. Some cumbersome tasks like harvesting and food preparation were once performed by neighborhood work parties; neighborhood women now rarely undertake them. And yet the underlying premise remains: that women are the preponderant force in both the household and the neighborhood. Women's behavior, as men and women see it, still largely determines either unit's corporateness, in the sense of its health or demise; for both units, in one way or another, still provide women with their primary social world, whether it be one from which to flee or one to inhabit.

FORCE AND PERSUASION

The separation of the sexes in Taroudannt society and the form of male dominance within it carry implications about the role that ideology plays in the continued subordination of Roudaniy women. Segregated from men in many facets of their lives, women are directly supervised and controlled by men relatively seldom. As a result, supervision of women is most often carried out by women or through restraints that women impose upon themselves. Women's self-image and their images of their own and the other sex emerge as crucial in perpetuating women's subordination.

As in other inegalitarian situations, control over Roudaniy women is exercised through force to a degree. There is the force of law, as men and other women charge and punish recalcitrant women for socially unacceptable acts. There is also the force of physical coercion, as men corporally punish women for not conforming to custom or to men's individual decrees. A husband has the legal right to beat his wife, for example: the only restriction is that he should not inflict excessive punishment. And there is the political and economic power which men hold over the women that they represent and support: most women remain economic dependents throughout the greater parts of their lives, use men as their legal spokesmen, and so are beholden to them.

Thus Taroudannt women often feel compelled to conform to a male dominance system through fear of some form of reprisal. To the degree that others might discover or punish their insubordination, these are appropriate responses. To the degree that exposure is not anticipated, however, women's compliance seems to have other roots. Since sex segregation lessens the likelihood of discovery, an added level of control appears operative and is constituted by women's belief in female inferiority and the appropriateness of women's subordination.

At issue is the control of women's and men's minds. Believing in their own inferiority, Moroccan women hem in their own sex. They limit other women's freedoms through a fear of women's excesses, and sometimes court men's approval by reporting women's misdeeds. And if women apply these constraints upon other women, they often extend them to themselves quite as stringently. Ironically, even when a woman succeeds in curbing her own freedoms to such a degree that she conforms to the ultimate female ideal, her very feat is taken as proof of womankind's innate inferiority, as much as of womankind's capability, by virtue of its rarity. The Taroudannt woman remains maligned, as will be seen.

Chapter Three

BEYOND
THE WESTERN STEREOTYPE

W hat is the Arab-Muslim woman in the eyes of her compatriots? The question calls to mind myriad images of how Arab-Muslim men and women are said to view her. There is the Western stereotype of the Arab man sequestering his woman in a harem, forcing a life of purdah upon her, and otherwise dooming her to exist veiled in body and spirit. Westerners are apt to read much about notions of superiority and inferiority into their portrayal. Too, there is the associated image provided by many social reformers, Western and non-Western: for them, the Arab-Muslim woman is sometimes angry, sometimes naïve and submissive, but in all events shackled. By virtue of her history, if not her innate nature, she must be moved into a more public world. There is also the image of the strong-minded and manipulative Middle Eastern woman, maneuvering in the family sphere with her informal powers and her marked self-assurance. This image of covert power has been stressed by certain outsiders and also has its own long-standing place within the societies involved. And there is the portrayal that Muslim devouts sometimes offer, one that depicts women as equal to men in the eyes of Allah, a notion that they forward as truly Islamic on the basis of certain religious writings.

These views, some imputed to and some offered by Arab-Muslims, provide a congeries of often contradictory images. They involve potent, rather stark depictions which, while confronting the sexual issue, more nearly gear themselves to other tasks, important among them being their use as one kind of weaponry in broader political debates. Contemporary Westerners are likely to point to the image of female inferiority that they see in the harem stereotype, thereby drawing support for the notion that Western culture and more specifically Western attitudes about sex and women are more progressive. The stance is an old one: as a response to a growing nationalism, for example, colonialist administrators evoked the image of the veiled Arab-Muslim woman as proof of the need for a civilizing mission from outside. The admirer of Arab-Muslim culture, insider or outsider, by contrast, often gravitates toward the image of the powerful female: he or she is likely to use it to counteract a Western-based perception of Arab tyranny and backwardness. And the contemporary Muslim scholar, for his part, might emphasize certain facets of the image that Islam forwards about women in order to sustain his own Islamizing crusade by showing that his religion is ''modern,'' fair-minded, and egalitarian.

Colonialism, nationalism, pan-Arabism, pan-Islam, and, of course, feminism and antifeminism: all these phenomena have generated their descriptions of and commentaries about male-female relations in the Arab-Muslim world, and more particularly about the status of Arab-Muslim women. One can only conjecture upon the reasons for this powerful interest in the face of what are often broader concerns: is it due to the seductiveness of the sequestered Arab-Muslim woman, to the basic lure of primordial womanhood which is in all events intriguing, or to a more conscious strategy on the part of outsiders to reduce a complex society to its female aspect, one of its less heralded parts? As Fanon (1966) suggests for the Algerian case, all these have had their part in forming the vivid images that Europeans hold of Algerian women, as Algerian men are said to view them. And as Laroui (1967) has noted, the Arab-Muslim has often answered in the same terms, occasionally using his own sleight-of-hand, by arguing the subordination of European women: "he knows well that the rights of women are sacrificed in Islam, at least in practice. But how will he resist the pleasure of making use of the Villermé report and of other critical writings on the exploitation of feminine work?" (Laroui 1967: 39).

Object of countless portrayals, the Arab-Muslim woman, as subject, too often becomes lost in the artfulness of these debates. She comes to be described in extremes, sometimes even within the same line of argument. "Inert object" (Fanon 1966: 23) in the eyes of the French colonialist, she nonetheless was also taken to be the prime social mover, to such a degree that considerable money and energy were allocated in North Africa to the task of winning over women, for surely "the rest would follow" (Fanon 1966: 23).

This French colonial formula for cultural conquest merged two opposing images, those of the Arab-Muslim woman as active and passive, all the while obscuring the more meaningful reality of how Arab-Muslim women blend the two or are believed to blend the two in the eyes of their men. This focus upon simplifications and extremes, which the colonial ground plan crystallizes within itself, tends to be writ large in the many debates about how these women are regarded societally. Many social commentators (e.g., Antoun 1968; Granqvist 1931; Pruvost 1974) have presented Arab-Muslim beliefs in terms of a male-superior, female-inferior paradigm. "Islam looks upon women with an unfriendly and suspicious eye," says Westermarck (1930: 65). "It pronounces their general depravity to be much greater than that of men. According to Muhammadan tradition the Prophet said: 'I have not left any calamity more hurtful to man than woman . . . O assembly of women, give alms, although it be of your gold and silver ornaments: for verily you are mostly of hell on the day of resurrection.' And women are stupid and ignorant as well as wicked." According to the schema, women are deemed less intelligent, less rational, more emotional, and more vengeful than men. Other theorists (see below) forward the opposing view: within Arab-Muslim societies, they say, women are not viewed as inferior nor men as superior; rather the sexes maintain a certain equality in Arab-Muslim eyes, because of Allah's putatively equal estimation of them. "Women are the sisters of men," states one tradition of the Prophet which such Muslims are wont to cite; "they assume the same obligations and enjoy the same rights." And if equality would seem to be the ultimate stance to which the deniers of an ethic of female inferiority might strive, still others assert that Muslims credit women with a greater power than men hold. Mernissi (1975), for example, suggests that a belief in women's potent, seductive sexuality and in men's sexual vulnerability leads Muslim society to keep the sexes apart and women in seclusion so that a religious attitude might be encouraged. She concludes that this practice reveals a recognition of women's overriding power: she says that no ideology of female inferiority exists in Morocco or more generally in Islamic society, past or present.

Since Arab society takes Islam as its conceptual core, much of the evidence that has been marshaled toward these diverse ends has involved religious tenets. Proponents of the view that Arab-Muslim women are perceived and treated as inferiors note that women are regarded as dependents and minors according to the traditional law, which is religious in basis. In the Koran, men are called upon to be "the managers of the affairs of women" and are encouraged to "admonish, banish . . . to their couches, and beat" those women whom men "fear may be in rebellion" (Arberry 1955: I, 105 f.). They are designated as women's sexual guardians, the Koran providing these words of support:

And say to the believing women, that they   ✻
Cast down their eyes, and guard their
Private parts, and reveal not their adornment
Save such as is outward; and let them cast
Their veils over their bosoms, and not reveal
Their adornment save to their husbands,
Or their fathers, or their husbands' fathers,
Or their sons, or their husbands' sons,
Or their brothers, or their brothers' sons,
Or what their right hands own, or such men
As attend them, not having sexual desire,
Or children who have not yet attained knowledge
Of women's private parts, nor let them stamp
Their feet so that their hidden ornament may be known.
[Arberry 1955: 49f.]

actually does not say anything about the face

Defenders of the equality view acknowledge this caretakership, all the while emphasizing the heights to which women might rise within it. Both sexes, they argue, are regarded as essential parts of the earthly community of the faithful (Chabbi 1974: 551 f.), and both ultimately enjoy the same salvation if they believe. Both, in short, are equal in their socioreligious placement. Indeed, Islam, say most Muslims, provided women with new rights and safeguards and gave back her dignity (Sammari 1947: 551).

One does well to reweigh this evidence and before it, to reexamine the debaters' lines; for the frame of reference, if not the particulars of the debate, has largely been a Western one, through the use of which many essentials of Arab-Muslim sexual attitude have been lost. In essence, the proponents of Western culture have attacked from their own perspective, while the proponents of Arab-Muslim culture have shaped the broad strokes of their rejoinder essentially in their opponents' terms. Some critics are wont to see this as indicative of the mentality of the colonized (Laroui 1974); others might see it more nearly as a natural exigency of debate. Whatever the origins, however, the broad outlines of the argument tend to obscure, while the finer points of the dialogue reveal facets of a belief structure about sexuality that is at variance with the Western framework. These facets call for a consideration divorced from the Western model and in their own terms. The Arab-Muslim Mohamed Sammari, for example, speaks about womankind as she exists at her creation, during her earthly life, and in paradise. Is this merely a sign of religious attitude, as Westerners might interpret it, or does it reveal a crucial Arab-Muslim linkage, sexuality as joined to temporality? The Arab-Muslim man should admonish, manage his woman's affairs, and guard against her rebellion: do these Koranic admonitions point to a somewhat different perception of activity and passivity than that projected by the French administrator-colonist? The Koran asserts regarding the two sexes: "God in bounty has preferred one of them over another" (Arberry 1955: I, 105). A Westerner is apt to deduce that men are deemed superior by virtue of the assertion, and yet the determinants of male superiority, if indeed there be an Arab-Muslim notion of male superiority pure and simple, are notably lacking in the formulation. One must go back to the Arab-Muslim side of the discourse and ask if such determinants exist, and if so, then why?

PRELIMINARY PERSPECTIVES

Let us begin at the beginning with Adam and Eve. The three tales that follow are recounted by many Moroccans, male and female, to explain current custom and to define differences in men's and women's drives and their impact upon behavior. They are creation myths in that they recount the origins of humankind or society. They depict more than the simple creation, however, for Adam and Eve display certain potentialities, apparently unintuited even by Allah, once the two sexes are placed upon the earth. In his attempt to deal with these characterological tendencies, Allah lays down certain organizational principles, and culture emerges along with society, still in its basic outlines but chiefly as a constraint.

Tale 1: The First Lie

When Allah put Adam and Eve in the Garden, he lowered bread and grapes to them, so that each would have something to eat. Adam and Eve were still alone at that time, had not yet met, and had not had sexual relations. Each day, however, Adam would eat and then would start searching for Eve, looking all day and sleeping at night. Eve looked day and night for Adam, and never rested. Finally, Adam found Eve. He went to her and said, "I have been looking for you each day; have you also been looking for me?" Eve answered that she had remained always in one place and had not moved from it. The first lie was born from the coyness of Eve.

Tale 2: Inheritance

Each day that Adam and Eve were still in the Garden, an angel sent down half a bread and some grapes to each of the two. When alone, each ate alone. Once Adam and Eve had met, however, Eve continued to eat hers alone, while Adam gave half his bread to his companion. When Allah saw the injustice, he punished women. He gave women only half of what men received in inheritance, for women had taken the extra half that men had chosen to provide.

Tale 3: Eve's Children

Thereafter Adam and Eve slept together, and Eve gave birth to twins in succession. Of each set of twins, one was exceptionally beautiful and one was only relatively so. Each time, Eve took the more beautiful one and hid it underground to be hers alone. She presented only the somewhat beautiful ones to Adam.

One day, Adam sensed that there might be more children and went out to Eve. He questioned her. She lied, however, saying that the children he had seen were the only ones that existed. He asked her again, and again she lied to him. Finally he asked a third time, commanding her to swear on her future. At that, Eve revealed the children hidden below. And it was prophesied that the children from below would hurt the children of above. The ones below, meager, thin, and fragile from their separation, would become the *jnun* (underworld spirits) and would strike down the children from above in revenge for their imprisonment. They would cause them sickness and pain. Since children are the most precious thing for any woman, the discovery and removal of the beautiful ones served as Eve's punishment.

The immediate overriding message of these tales is that women are morally inferior to men. Indeed, at the most manifest level, the creation tales support the model for Arab-Muslims' sexuality that most Westeners project onto them. Eve lies and cheats and proves herself to be selfish and frivolous; Adam eventually demonstrates his rectitude by calling on Allah and by showing social concern. Through the behavior of both individuals, the male-female interchange takes on an oppositional dynamic.

This correspondence—man positive, woman negative—is frequent in much casual conversation among Moroccans. A Moroccan man might say that his wife is akin to a cow, referring at once to her limited responsibility and her animality, or he might say that an old female neighbor shares her brains with an ass, half and half. Similarly, a woman might point to the vulnerability and treachery of the women around her and might even cite these same characteristics in describing her own behavior. Generalizations of a positive sort, to the extent that these are forthcoming, tend to focus on men.

And yet other possibilities emerge through a closer analysis of the Adam and Eve tales and through a more extended consideration of Moroccans' spontaneous discourse. Adam and Eve come to exhibit opposing qualities as they interact, but as importantly, they are initially neutral when they are first placed in the Garden.

Both are untainted, without original sin, as Muslims avow, and as a result, both are initially free from God-imposed burdens and restrictions. Indeed, Adam and Eve first live in a state of equality: their daily portions of food are equal and are delivered directly, without intermediaries. At that first moment, womankind is in no way a minor, dependent, or subordinate in the eyes of Allah.

The message of the innate inferiority of women is also tempered in Moroccans' conversations. Verbal denigration of women, for example, is not typically extended to all womankind. Rather it centers upon women in the states of marriage, divorce, and widowhood. As a category, young girls are seldom portrayed in a negative light. By extension, affirmations of male superiority most often concern mature men, while the characterizations of younger males tend to be negative.

Thus an adult-nonadult distinction might profitably be added to the male-female one in order to move toward a closer rendition of how Moroccans distribute positive and negative traits between men and women. The representations found in a variety of Moroccan discourses, however, still do not parcel themselves out neatly when viewed in these terms. The behaviors attributed to males and females in Moroccan folklore, for example, do not neatly fit the male-positive, female-negative model even for the adult subgroup. If Moroccan women are often depicted as more passionate, more vengeful, less responsible, and more crafty, Moroccan men are frequently portrayed as uncontrolled, unforgiving, foolhardy, and deceitful. Indeed, some of the folk literature's more pungent representations of character weakness involve adult men.

Tale 4: The Two Woodgatherers

There once were two old men who worked at woodgathering. Each day they went out to the forest together. Tired and dirty, they would return together at the end of the day. On Fridays, however, one woodgatherer did not go out to work. Instead he washed himself and his clothing at the bath and proceeded to the mosque. The other woodgatherer had no thought of the mosque and prepared himself ritually in no way.

On Friday, at the congregational service, the *imam* (prayer leader) sneezed and the first woodgatherer said "God bless you." The *imam* took note of it. Later the mosque's pulpit broke and the first woodgatherer came to help fix it, without being asked. The *imam* called to the man and gave him a lapful of silver in thanks.

Seeing the luck of his partner, the second woodgatherer resolved to act like him. That Friday, he washed and went to the mosque. But the *imam* did not sneeze. Once he cleared his throat, to which the second woodgatherer responded "God bless you." The *imam* sneered and took note of it. Then he waited for the pulpit to break, but it did not. So he broke it, and offered to repair it in turn.

The police went to the *imam* and reported that a woodgatherer had broken the pulpit. Knowing only one woodgatherer, the one that he once had rewarded, the *imam* concluded that the man had become uppity and called the first woodgatherer to him. When the police summoned the first, however, the second came running. They beat him and put him in jail.

By extension, while adult female character is often portrayed as negative, women nonetheless do not lack positive representation in the folkloric materials. The tale of the woodgatherer's wife (tale 5) demonstrates that women are believed able to fulfill men's expectations for their sex. Similarly, the tale of the lapidation (tale 6) demonstrates that women can exhibit generalized human virtues. In the first tale, the wife is obedient, self-sacrificing, and totally submissive. In the second tale, the heroine is magnanimous, faithful, and sexually controlled. Few male folk characters, apart from the male saints, can match that woman in her compassion and openheartedness.

Tale 5: The Wife of the Woodgatherer

The wife of the woodgatherer had a husband whom she respected. Each day, when he went off to the forest, she took her broom and stood in the courtyard in the sun (for he worked in the sun and she did not wish to be better off than he was). She did not enter their room until the close of the day. One day the Prophet sent Lalla Fatima Zahara, his daughter, to visit. She knocked at the door. "Who is it?" the wife of the woodgatherer asked. "Lalla Fatima Zahara, the daughter of the Prophet. Let me in." "I must ask my husband" was the response. "Come back tomorrow." That night the wife consulted with her husband. "Lalla Fatima Zahara, the daughter of the Prophet, came to the door today. Should I let her in?" "Let her in," he said.

The next day, Lalla Fatima Zahara returned, this time with Hsen (the firstborn of her twins). She knocked. "Who is it?" asked the wife of the woodgatherer. "Lalla Fatima Zahara, the daughter of the Prophet, and Hsen. Let us in." "I asked about Lalla Fatima Zahara, but I did not ask about Hsen. I must ask my husband. Come back tomorrow." That night the wife of the woodgatherer asked and he said "Let them in."

A third time, Lalla Fatima Zahara knocked at the door, and the wife of the woodgatherer answered, "Who is it?" "Lalla Fatima Zahara, Hsen, and Hussein (the second-born twin). Let us in." "I asked about Lalla Fatima Zahara, daughter of the Prophet, and Hsen, but not Hussein. I must ask my husband. Come back tomorrow." A third time she asked and the husband said "Let them in."

The next day Lalla Fatima Zahara knocked at the door, and the wife of the woodgatherer let her into their room. There she saw three mattresses. And Lalla Fatima Zahara asked, "Whose are these mattresses?" for the couple had no children and lived alone. And the wife of the woodgatherer responded, "The right one is mine, as is the left one, while the middle one is my husband's. When my husband lies down, I light a candle until sleep has taken him. Then I extinguish it and lie down. And when he sleeps on his left side, I sleep on the right mattress, and when he turns onto his right side, I move to the left mattress, so as always to face him." Lalla Fatima Zahara then returned to her home, understanding why she had been sent.

Tale 6: The Lapidation

There once was a judge whose brother went on the pilgrimage, leaving his wife home alone. The judge desired his sister-in-law, and so one day sent his servant with a gift for her. His brother's wife turned away the servant and sent back the present. The judge, however, would not be refused. That night he himself went to his brother's house and asked if he might enter. His sister-in-law sent him away also, berating him for his wantonness.

The next day, the judge told his neighbors that his brother's wife was a prostitute. He incited the people so that they rose up against her. They put her into a clearing and stoned her until stones covered her body. Then they left her for dead.

That evening a man rode by the pile of stones and heard someone inside of it, moaning. He cleared away the stones, found the woman, and took her to his home. There his wife treated her and cared for her. That same night the sister-in-law told them both about the injustice she had sustained.

On the day of the stoning, the judge succumbed to a grave illness. Sores covered his body that no one could cure. From that day, too, his sister-in-law found that she could cure people. The sick were brought to her from far and wide in order to be treated. In fact, her curing was so successful that the man of the house stopped working, for the money that the curer earned supported the three adults.

Several months later, the woman's husband returned from the pilgrimage. He found his brother ill and asked what had happened. The judge answered, "A misery." The judge then asked why his brother had not inquired about his wife. The pilgrim responded, "I asked about my brother, not my wife. If she is here, that is good. If she is gone, well then good-bye to her." To this the judge explained that the people had stoned her because of her wrongdoing.

The pilgrim took his brother to many curers, but the brother would not be cured. Finally, he heard of the woman who cured people. He wrapped his brother in wool, placed him on a stretcher, and brought him to the woman who still was his wife.

And when the curer cured, she sat behind a curtain. And when the sick were brought to her, she always attended to her patients alone. When the judge appeared, however, she asked both him and her husband to remain on the other side of the curtain. Then she asked the judge to confess his sins if he wanted to regain his health.

The judge protested, "I have done nothing, nothing." When she asked him a second time, he again refused to confess. Finally, the pilgrim implored his sick brother, saying that relief was worth any confession. To that, the judge responded, "I had the people stone your wife without reason." With that, the curer pulled back the curtain and made herself known to them. She added that she would cure his brother at her husband's request. The husband told her to cure him and then took his wife back to his home.

Already in these examples the breadth of behaviors attributable to men and women is apparent. The pilgrim is compassionate, while the judge is treacherous; the first woodgatherer is responsible and helpful, while the second is callous and self-serving. Similarly, the curer and the wife of the woodgatherer stand in sharp opposition to the Eve of creation. In the folktales virtue has its negative correlate in men, much as weakness has its positive correlate in women.

If male and female folk characterizations are not nearly so well defined as one might expect according to a male-positive, female-negative premise, neither does behavior cluster statistically around superior male and inferior female images. While male and female representations do differ in their distributions, that difference does not support a dichotomy of this kind. Instead there is more nearly an overlap of dominant characteristics. Thus when the behavior of folkloric characters is charted according to the presence or absence of valued characteristics for each sex (see table 3.1), women are indeed more often described as evil, possessive, deceitful, and lascivious. But men's behavior also falls within the negative half of the characterological spectrum: more male folk characters are foolish, selfish, and rapacious than are moral, openhearted, upstanding, and controlled.

Table 3.1 Character Traits in Folkloric Figures

	Positive	Negative	Neutral
Men	40 (43%)	47 (50%)	7 (7%)
Women	30 (32%)	59 (63%)	4 (4%)

These findings are interesting in that they describe the human condition as most adult Moroccans are wont to perceive it. In the Moroccan scheme of things, the truly virtuous are few, with some being men and some women. The majority of men, like the majority of women, are believed to be self-centered individuals who do not hesitate to do wrong if it is personally advantageous. Even male saints, being at once human and divine, occasionally reveal tendencies of an egotistical sort (tale 23).

STASIS RECONSIDERED

If adult men, like adult women, generally fall to the debit side with regard to their moral attributes, how does male dominance and female subordination come to be validated? Are men still regarded as morally ascendant, and if they are, then on what basis? How, in fact, do Moroccans rationalize the delegation of authority to the male sex?

The answers to these questions become clear, I believe, when it is realized that a major attribute of the Taroudannt characterizations of male and female is the temporal movement which is implicit in the Sammari argument rather than static binary opposition. Characters develop and situations change, and the form of the development contains crucial ideological messages. By focusing upon the unchangeable, the Western critic has generally missed the significance of this temporality in the Arab-Muslim schema. By considering only certain points in the developmental sequence, the denier of Arab-Muslim sexual inequality has generally neglected the message of female inferiority that the developmental process contains.

Moroccan sexual ideology in the Taroudannt form is more nearly an ideology of becoming than an ideology of being. Characters gain or lose ground with regard to the exhibition of basic

Moroccan virtues that remain ideals for Moroccan men and women. They consist, first, of the five Muslim religious duties, or *fruḍ:* the profession of faith in Allah and the Prophet, the doing of the daily prayers, the giving of alms and the tithe, submission to the month-long Ramadan fast, and when possible, the undertaking of the holy pilgrimage. Second, they concern honesty in its verbal and behavioral forms, the transgression of which is said to be particularly punished in the God-fearing: the beads of the brotherhood rosary, for example, are said to turn into a snake in the hands of him who dares to lie or cheat. Third, there are the family virtues: marital fidelity (which remains an ideal for men while constituting a stringent requirement for women), filial obedience, virginal purity, and the obligation of the head of the household to provide for his family's support. Fourth, there are the social virtues which maintain and smooth important interpersonal relations outside the family: a lack of covetousness, and if not forgiveness, then the ability to control vengeful feelings so that important social linkages will not be endangered. For women, the peculiarly female virtues of patience, modesty, and obedience define a fifth set of behavioral expectations.

As an ideology of becoming, Moroccan sexual ideology focuses upon how individual character changes or can change with respect to the incidence of these moral qualities. Its message concerns relative morality more than absolute goodness, and so expresses itself as a vector relation. Women—perhaps virtuous, perhaps wavering, perhaps evil—fall into greater disrepute as they act out their innermost tendencies. At their best, they might avoid the fall, but in few cases do they show evidence of enlightenment. Men—perhaps sinful, perhaps wavering, perhaps virtuous—become more respectable with time. If they do not exhibit improvement, still their morality does not diminish. Table 3.2, based upon the 95 Taroudannt folktales, demonstrates the recurrence of these two developmental patterns.

Table 3.2 Character Change in Folkloric Figures

	Positive Development	No Development	Negative Development
Men	25 (31%)	52 (64%)	4 (5%)
Women	4 (4%)	52 (56%)	37 (40%)

These two vector components are nicely juxtaposed in the tale of Our Saint Jesus. The wife in the tale is at first highly valued by her husband, for she is modest and obedient. Indeed, their marriage has a storybook flavor, both partners cherishing one another up to and after death. Her fall occurs late, but then its lateness also implies that life itself might be too short to encompass the male-female dynamic. Ironically, the wife's earthly life remains exemplary, but her negative potentiality is actualized after her death.

not "Jesus" as we know

Tale 7: Our Saint Jesus

There once was a husband who loved his wife mightily, and she in her turn obeyed and respected him. One day, the husband said to his wife, "Let us make a pact. If I die, you must promise not to marry again." And she too made him promise that he would not remarry if she were first to die. Finally, one day she died. Remembering his vow, the husband did not remarry, but instead sat at her grave, mourning her death.

One day, Our Saint Jesus walked by. He asked the man what he was doing, for in winter, spring, summer, and autumn the husband sat by his wife's grave. He never moved, and ate only the green that grew round him. To that, the man recounted his pact. Our Saint Jesus responded: "Get up and marry." But the man answered "No," that the vow had been made.

Seven years later, Our Saint Jesus walked by again. He found the man still mourning. Again he said, "Get up and remarry." But again the man said "No," that he would remain there until he and his wife were reunited. Hearing that, Our Saint Jesus brought the wife back to life.

The couple went off. Then the wife sat down, leaving her husband to sleep with his head on her thigh. There he slept a sleep that he hadn't slept in seven years.

While the husband was asleep, however, the son of the Sultan rode by. He saw the couple and neared them. Seeing the woman, he asked her, "Why do you stay with such a man (for he was ill-kempt from his vigil). Come with me instead, and I will give you gold and fine clothing." "All right," answered the woman. Taking a stone, she moved her husband's head from her lap over onto it, and went off.

When the man awakened, he found that his wife was gone. He searched far and wide to find her. Finally, he met the son of the Sultan and told him that he was looking for his wife, whom Our Saint Jesus had resurrected. The Sultan's son answered that he had not seen her, but that he would let the man see all of his wives and concubines (for he feared Jesus' wrath).

Hearing this news, the wife dressed so that no one would know her. But of the eighty or so women, she was immediately recognized. Confronted by her husband, she then denied that she was his wife. She called him simpleminded. "No," said the husband adamantly, "it is you that I married and who subsequently died."

Husband and wife went to Our Saint Jesus in order to resolve the dispute. In front of the saint, both swore to their veracity. Finally, Our Saint Jesus said that he needed to look at the grave. Once there, he asked the woman to step into the grave in order to test the size of it. The saint then covered over the opening and left the woman for dead.

With that, Our Saint Jesus again approached the husband. This time, the man was ready to listen. The saint told him to forget his wife and remarry, which the husband subsequently did.

The directional dynamic apparent in the tale of Our Saint Jesus is emphasized in numerous tales through the use of certain literary devices. One of these—the mechanism of the three trials—is evident in the tale of Eve's children (tale 3) and the lapidation (tale 6), as well as in the tale of Our Saint Jesus (tale 7). Here, the number three is associated with character revelation, as it is generally in the Semitic world, its usage being apparent in such New Testament accounts as Simon Peter's threefold rejection of his Lord and the third-day resurrection of Jesus. In the Tarou-dannt materials, evil or goodness frequently beckons on three separate occasions, with the third confrontation inducing character change. Again, male and female behaviors exhibit an oppositional dynamic: male characters tend to actualize their moral strength on the third occasion while women ultimately succumb to temptation.

A similar message is conveyed through the patterning of interactions involving same-sexed characters of different age and experience. Of such pairs, the older woman is generally the more wicked (64 percent) while the older man is more godly and upstanding (82 percent). Moreover, individuals of different ages are not juxtaposed merely to heighten the moral contrast; they interrelate catalytically: the older woman tends to lead the younger into temptation, while the older man tends to provide moral guidance. Significantly, even the mother is included in this set of negatively impelled older women.

Tale 8: The Lamb's Hocks

There once was a man who had a wife, and the wife had a mother. Each night when the man returned from work, he brought home a kilo of meat and a pair of lamb's hocks. Each night he told the wife that he would dine on the hocks, while she and her mother could eat all the meat. He cautioned, however, that the women should not take even a taste of the lamb's hocks, for this would lead to his death.

The wife prepared the hocks for him each day according to his command. One day, however, the wife's mother said, "Oh Lord, I must have a taste of those lamb's hocks." But the wife repeated her husband's words and refused. A few days passed, and again the wife's mother said that she wanted a taste of the lamb's hocks. Again the wife refused. Then finally the wife's mother demanded a third time. The wife answered, "There is a kilo of meat for us to eat. What is the need?" But the mother continued: "And if your husband dies, what is the loss? There are so many men in the world. Let him die from it." And so the wife cut two pieces from the hocks and set out the rest.

That night the husband returned home, looked at the hocks, and keeled over, as if dead. The wife called for the holy men to wash him and wrap him in the death shroud. Then the holy men placed him in a casket and carried him off. Not a tear was shed. As the procession passed the neighborhood store, however, and the owner asked who had died, the man jumped out of the coffin. He cursed his wife and her mother. Then he went off to the court and secured a divorce.

IRREVERSIBILITY

The tendency toward a developmental directionality is joined to an emphasis upon irreversibility, not only in the representation of the dynamics of male and female character but also in the conceptualization of development of other kinds. Both tendencies are revealed as interlinked, for example, in Moroccans' perceptions and practices of child rearing. Children can be weaned at various ages, but once weaned, they never again should be nursed. The infant is believed to suffer irreparably if regression is permitted. Similarly, toilet-training at first is characterized by relative permissiveness, but once a pattern of continence is established, mishaps are met with corporal punishment and angry words. At that point, parents and onlookers allow little flexibility, even though regression might be temporary, an immediate response to crisis.

The responses of the two women Hada and Taja to the misfortunes of Hada's two-year-old daughter are illustrative here. Hada had borne two children, the first having died essentially through her carelessness, while the second also suffered: the child was left dirty, was dragged from house to house, and was periodically covered with sores. By contrast, Taja, her neighbor, had borne a daughter after having been barren for five years. She was an extremely conscientious mother, to the point of being overly solicitous. It was Taja who more than anyone had kept Hada's child alive during its traumatic first years.

One day, Hada visited with her daughter at her hand. The little girl was feverish and cranky. Hada commented that the child had been ill, pulling it to her side as she settled in, awaiting afternoon tea. Suddenly there was a swish of liquid and the quick realization that the little girl had urinated and defecated. Screams were heard from both women. Hada tiraded about her daughter's shameful childishness, punctuating her words with two hard whacks, a twisted ear, and much pushing and shoving. Taja, too, berated the child: "Are you a baby that you do this in others' homes? Have you not learned?" And then she proceeded to vent her outrage upon the mother: "Why do you venture out with such a child?" The outburst was the most heated that I had ever seen from that normally even-tempered woman.

Frenzied reactions in such circumstances seem to be tied to a culturally constituted fear that regression augurs enduring loss. Dire effects are felt to ensue, for example, from resumed suckling of a child; the infant's death is expected unless countermagic is utilized, with such countermagic being viewed as often inadequate. Moreover, tragic effects ensue even should the child nurse at the mother's breast mistakenly. In order to guard against this eventuality, mothers often wear sweaters that close up the back when they sleep during the weaning days.

In a sharply different vein, the equation of irreversible action with proper action is believed to have affected the options of the Prophet. Even certain patterns frivolously or mistakenly formulated in the Prophet's name emerge as inviolate, and so continue to elicit godly support for their maintenance. The Jews fast one day; the Muslims one month. Each human must die, but cannot rise to life on this earth again. As the following tales demonstrate, these patterns are perpetuated, despite the inconvenience and pain that they cause, because their initial occurrence has transformed them into unchangeable cultural realities.

Islamic only law is only a possibility ~ *don't challenge*

Mohammed decides

Tale 9: The Afterlife

After Lalla Fatima Zahara, daughter of the Prophet, had borne Hsen and Hussein, the Prophet asked her: "When people die, will they come back to life on this earth again?" And his daughter answered without hesitation: "No. They will not live again. They will seize the ground." Later when her own son died, Lalla Fatima Zahara asked her father to resurrect him. But the Prophet replied, "The first word, in it is blessing." Thereafter neither her dead son nor other humans were brought back to life.

Tale 10: Ramadan

The chimpanzee was originally *mwa 'aguz,* an old woman and messenger for the Prophet. When the Prophet had messages to transmit, he would send her, for she did not lie. One day, the Prophet sent her to the Jews and the Muslims with decrees about the fast. He commanded her: "Tell the Jews to fast one month the size of a fingernail, and tell the Muslims to fast one day the size of a pinkynail." But the old woman reversed the messages, telling the Jews to fast one day and the Muslims one month. When she realized her error, she ran to the Prophet. He, however, left her words unaltered. In punishment, however, he transformed her— turned her into a chimpanzee—which is how she remains.

COMPLEMENTARITY

With regard to the narrower issue of male-female relations, complementarity joins directionality and irreversibility as an attribute of the sexual developmental framework. Goodness, as has been seen, is not an exclusively male attribute, nor does it exist without its counterpart, evil. Indeed, and paradoxically, whereas men move toward goodness and virtue through striving and effort, seldom achieving it, women are more nearly endowed with a degree of moral fiber which only certain of Morocco's more assiduous men are believed able to match. Women are born with it to a degree, unknowingly cultivate it, and then, when men are most apt to attain it, women find that it is lacking.

At birth, it is said, women have one hundred angels and men have one hundred devils. Each year, however, one angel moves from the female to the male and one devil moves from the male to the female until male virtue and female folly reach their ultimate actualizations. There is a moral transformation which causes a reversal in character if not a reversal in roles. The transformation is also expressed in a more prosaic, down-to-earth version by rural Moroccans. Man starts out life with one hundred worms or *dud*. Yearly, one worm passes to the woman until the man finds himself pure. For the woman, life brings moral and physical degradation. Interestingly, the proverb of the angels and devils is found not only in the south of Morocco but also in Morocco's north (Westermarck 1930: 68; Vinogradov 1974) and among the Algerians (Gaudry 1928: 267).

Whether it is found in its elegant or its mundane version, the aphorism of the devils not only substantiates the directional nature of maleness and femaleness; it also stresses the additional premise that maleness and femaleness are continually intertwined. Femaleness, says the aphorism, cannot be understood without maleness, much as goodness cannot be understood without evil. The male-female interchange induces a qualitative and quantitative moral interrelation.

The limited good notion of goodness and evil that the aphorism forwards implies that the intertwining of the sexes must be of a particularly pessimistic sort: men and women must live in ongoing interactive tension, for each sex forms a primary threat to the other, in that each threatens to occasion the loss of the other's positive attributes. Nor is the joint perfection of the sexes logically possible: this realization constitutes the belief system's enduringly cynical undercurrent.

Chapter Four

FROM GIRL TO WOMAN

A woman is like an apricot,
Eighteen days and she is out of season.
                                              Moroccan proverb

THE CRISIS OF DEFLORATION

There are many meanings and emotions associated with the word *bint* in Morocco. *Bint* is "daughter" and carries with it the range of emotions relevant to what parents feel for their children, most important being love. *Bint* is also a marker of descent, a Moroccan female being called *bint* with reference to her father; she is, for example, legally and formally Fatima bint Muhammad, Fatima daughter of Muhammad, with the honor or dishonor of the family being contained in the assignation. Character can also be implied depending upon how the term is employed: a woman is called *bint n-nas* (daughter of the people) if she is open and friendly or *bint l-ḥram* (daughter of the forbidden) if she is wicked. Yet another meaning of the term is "girl," "female child," or "someone female but not yet adult," which carries with it the protectiveness that adults extend to the still helpless. *Wa bniti* (O my little girl) is said to a loved one, a female of whatever age, whom one wishes to guide through concern and affection.

Perhaps the most complex use of the term *bint,* however, is still another: it is "virgin." *Bint* is a female who has not yet been deflowered. Here, the immediate determinant is a purely biological fact in which Moroccans show a marked interest. In Taroudannt, a wedding almost certainly provokes the query, "Was she a virgin?" meaning most simply, "Has she bled?" To Roudaniyin, this question is appropriate, for the simple biological fact carries with it many revelations. One intuits the depth of the concern when one hears even casual onlookers or passersby posing the defloration question. One gleans it, too, as scores of guests at a Moroccan wedding wait long hours for tangible proof or disproof of the fact. Gathered together in separate male and female groups since the early evening, a bride and groom's guests witness the arrival of the bride in the wee hours of the morning on the first day of the wedding week. Then the groom arrives and enters the bride's chamber, and the serious waiting begins. Gathered in the courtyard, the female guests await the bringing of the bride's blood-stained garment from the bridal room, which likely is adjacent to the court. Then, when the bride has proved to be deflowered, a servant woman dances into the crowd with the garment on a serving tray. The happy guests contribute money as they look at the stain. Through their witness, the honor of the bride and her family is protected. If there is no blood-stained garment, however, guests continue the vigil, occasional jibes being directed at the groom, a growing distrust being directed at the bride.

There is much anxiety over defloration even before marriage. Mothers sometimes check their daughters just before their wedding nights in order to make certain that their hymens are intact.

Or they might pay a doctor, who examines and then writes out a certificate of virginity for use in the event that the girl's purity should be questioned. In the latter instances, there is tension regarding the certificate itself, which can take on a symbolic character quite different from that which the doctor expects. In a sense, there is a sleight-of-hand. In a region in which the large majority of inhabitants are illiterate, some believe that virginity is substantiated or not according to the color of the doctor's writing. Red ink is felt to indicate danger, crisis, blood, and a broken hymen. Black indicates virginity, or so the bride's family says. Few, of course, are the doctors who are aware of this belief, and happily for most brides, many are the doctors who prefer black to red ink.

Complementary to the anxiety of the bride's family is the righteous anger that the groom's kinfolk should exhibit if defloration has occurred before the wedding night. A groom might display uncontrollable rage if he discovers that his putatively virginal bride is not a virgin. He might storm out of the bridal chamber and curse the bride and her family while pointing to the room, which a flock of women immediately enter. Thereupon the bride is immediately checked. Should her virginity still be in dispute, outside experts, old well-regarded women and/or Western-trained doctors, might be called in for their diagnoses. The girl's family might even remove her to the hospital in the dead of night in order to obtain a face-saving opinion. One recent bride was taken to one doctor by the groom's family and another doctor by her own family. Each was said to provide the witness that his clients needed and sought.

Anxiety and freneticism are appropriate on both sides, for the repercussions of a failed demonstration can be enormous for both bride and groom. There is the threat of economic loss, for a groom sometimes feels compelled through honor to cancel the wedding because of a bride's lack of virginity. Since both families have contributed heavily financially, both then suffer loss. For the bride the financial loss is even more far-reaching: legally a groom need not provide his wife with the customary compensation upon divorce if he can prove fraud. Moreover, since the bride's lack of virginity has become public knowledge through the scandal, the girl cannot afterward easily style herself a virgin. This fact can cause much hardship, for through the revelation her good reputation is largely lost. For his part, too, the groom confronts the likelihood of stigma. His guests chat, sometimes lasciviously, sometimes goodnaturedly, about the possibility of his impotence, while his near kin try to induce him to confess quickly should he be impotent and counteract the evil, embarrassing state. They bombard him with good advice and suggestions for cures and protection: there are incense, spices, and the ritual of passing him through his mother's robes, an act which symbolizes rebirth.

Fear of disaster is so marked regarding the defloration issue that numerous countermeasures have been developed regarding it. Substantial is the lore, for example, about how virginity can be faked. Pouches of chicken blood that burst in the vagina at the moment of penetration, the use of alum upon the vulva to tighten the vaginal opening, a quick cut of a razor—any conscientious mother will gladly use these techniques in order to protect her child's reputation. Indeed, it is the daughter who is nonvirginal and does not communicate it who causes her mother real discomfort and displeasure, not the honest and communicative nonvirginal child.

In turn, various precautions are taken on behalf of the virginal bride so that defloration is unequivocally proved. The ritual of defloration demands, for example, that the groom should break his bride's hymen on the wedding night and then immediately withdraw without ejaculation. There is no intercourse to completion for either husband or wife. In fact, it is shameful for the couple, and by extension, for the two families, if the virgin's bloodstained clothing—proof of her purity—should exhibit her husband's semen. Moroccans say that semen turns the red stain yellow, leading guests to believe that it has been caused by menstrual blood.

Ultimately, the emphasis is upon blood and a broken hymen rather than intercourse. Some customs, for example, point to the belief that a virgin will remain virginal in spirit even after having intercourse if her hymen remains intact. This state of physiological resilience is believed to be ritually attainable by passing a girl under a weaver's loom. In this way, the girl's hymen is felt to be reinforced so that if ever opened, it will quickly close in upon itself, as do weft and warp on the loom.

Many mothers are so eager that their daughters have this protection that the erection of a loom can become an important occasion for women. A woman weaver sometimes contacts female friends and neighbors, inviting interested mothers to bring their daughters to her when the loom goes up. She also might contact mothers whose protected daughters are soon to be wed. These girls must pass back under the loom a second time in order that the closing be removed for the wedding night, for the loom ritual is felt to be inimical to the consummation of marriage.

So certain are many women regarding the efficacy of this custom that they sometimes cite the passing of a girl under the loom as they provide assurance to a suitor's family that their daughter will be an uncompromised bride. "Yes, she has been seen with men, but we have passed her under a loom" is sometimes offered without shame or embarrassment. It is a logical although revealing comment; for both families, defloration must be avoided at all costs, or at the minimum hidden.

THE GOLDEN AGE OF VIRGINITY

The act of defloration is important for brides and grooms because it demonstrates that "the merchandise has not been used":

Moroccans state this explicitly and in precisely these terms. By
extension, the fact that "the merchandise has not been used"
implies a state of character and soul or the likelihood of it. Most
simply, virginity marks a time of purity and goodness in women.
The following tale indicates that age is largely irrelevant to this
formulation, nor is marital status a sufficient indicator. Instead it
implies that the likely source of one older, married woman's
continuing magnanimity lies in the virginity that others assume she
has lost.

Tale 11: The Virgin Widow

It is said that there once was a wealthy man, high in government
circles, who had taken a young bride and had subsequently lived
with her for twenty-five years without fathering children, or as
outsiders saw it, with her being barren. After those twenty-five
years of apparent conjugal harmony, during which the wife was
modest, upright, and obedient, the husband, who was considerably older than his wife, suddenly died. The wife returned to her
family and observed the appropriate period of mourning. Then
after a year she again was sought in marriage by a man of good
standing. A short, one-day wedding was planned, in keeping with
the bride-to-be's widowed (nonvirginal) status. On the wedding
day, however, as the court's representatives drew up the marriage
contract and then asked the bride for her consent—a technicality
within the system—the bride-to-be replied: "Do not give me the
contract of a *hejjala* (widow, nonvirgin) but rather that of a virgin."
For all of her married days, her husband had been impotent and
she had remained quiet. In keeping with her revelation, marriage
plans were revised, a full seven-day wedding was planned, and the
widow received the promise of a virgin's financial compensation. (It
should be added that the widow's behavior—her loyalty, her
modesty and her quiet acceptance of a stigmatizing childlessness—
were seen as representative of a virgin's behavior rather than that
of a sexually experienced wife.)

The virgin widow of the tale, likely aged about forty, exhibits
generally laudable behavior and epitomizes numerous virtues. In

many ways, however, foreshadowings of a similar perspicacity
can be expected from even very young girls. Four-year-old Titim
stood before this anthropologist and some kinswomen in a dress
that her father had just recently bought. She behaved shyly and
modestly, was thankful and expressed it, and, in all, evinced a
winning enthusiasm. She already had 'aqel (intelligence, responsibility), her aunt said as she viewed the child with pride.
"'Aquel?" I ventured, wondering about the attribution of intelligence to someone so young. Then the woman elaborated: children are sometimes said to begin showing 'aqel at age seven, the
time at which they formally enter school, but that is a mistaken
notion, for girls have intelligence, in the sense of social propriety,
often at a much younger age, while boys are lucky to develop it by
the age of twenty, should they develop it at all. With that, Titim's
aunt turned to her almost-adult yet still carefree son, as if to
underscore the comparison.

The following tale depicts the virtues of a still youthful virgin:
her naïve certainty, her unusual common sense, and her essential
wisdom, qualities through which she wins the admiration of two
well-regarded adult males.

Tale 12: The Quince

There was once a farmer whose quinces and figs ripened out of
season. He was a poor man and a widower, who lived with his
daughter, eking out a meager living. When he saw that his fruit
arrived out of season, he decided to take some to the Sultan,
hoping to gain a favor through the Sultan's grace. The farmer went
and filled a basket with the nicest of quinces, putting fresh grass on
top. Then he left to get his donkey, leaving the quinces in the
vestibule.

At the same time, the daughter was preparing the father's
morning soup. Seeing the basket, she inquired for whom the
quinces were destined. The father answered that they were for the
Sultan. Going off, the daughter filled a second basket with the best
of the figs that ripened out of season, also putting grass on top.

Then she went to her father, telling him to take only the figs to the Sultan. With the quinces, the women of the Sultan's house would first choose, cut, cook, and taste them, said she, and the Sultan would end up with only the last taste. With the figs, the Sultan would enjoy them completely, untouched. The father agreed, took the figs, and rode off.

The farmer's figs were brought to the Sultan. Seeing them, however, the Sultan got angry and called the farmer to him. "Others bring me gold and silver, and you bring only figs." As punishment the Sultan had the farmer tied and put him and the figs next to the servants' waterjug. The ruler decreed that whoever drank should punish the farmer by hitting him with a fig.

A while later, the guards reported that the farmer was muttering. Each time that a fig hit him, the farmer licked the mush off his face and ate (for no other food was provided for him), and each time he blessed his daughter. Hearing that, the Sultan became curious and called the farmer to him, asking what he had said. So the farmer explained how he had first packed the quinces, but how the daughter had said not to take them because the women of the household would take the first taste. And he added that if he had taken the quinces, he surely would have died when struck.

Seeing the wisdom of the girl, the Sultan took her as his wife, although he had never seen her. Her father became the father-in-law of the Sultan and so obtained considerable wealth.

In many ways, the virgin approximates the Moroccan female ideal. The irony is, however, that the virgin's deeds are likely to be ill-placed and ill-timed, albeit laudable. Ensconced in the home and dependent upon family, the virgin has few occasions to exhibit her resourcefulness. The daughter in the quince tale does so through the crisis of the first fruits; the adolescent girl who judges better than adult men do in the Moroccan version of the Merchant of Venice story (Scelles-Millie 1970: 32–47), finds her opportunity only because she masquerades as a male. In the Moroccan version of Hansel and Gretel, the situation is similar: the Moroccan Gretel teaches and protects her brother during their various trials, never leaving him, even when her own life is endangered; she manifests her positive potentialities, however, only because her parents' treachery forces a dramatic display.

Tale 13: The Boy and the Girl (Hansel and Gretel)

There was once a man and his wife, son, and daughter. Each day the man brought home two pigeons, one to be shared by him and his son, and the other to be shared by his wife and his daughter. One day, the wife said: "Why not leave our children in the wilderness? That way we each will have a whole pigeon."

The next day, the father took the boy and the girl to the forest. As they walked, the daughter ate dates and dropped the pits on the road. She walked and dropped a pit; she walked and dropped a pit. Finally, the three reached the depths of the wilderness, and the father left them to stay there alone. "Do not worry," he told them. "I will leave some wheat stalks hanging in that tree. When they rustle (and they inevitably would rustle because they would blow in the wind), you will know that I'm coming." With that, he was gone.

The children waited and waited. Although the wheat rustled, the father did not return. Finally the girl said, "Let us go home alone." With that, she searched for the date pits and followed them home.

Once at the door, the brother and sister heard their mother and father talking. "Now let us eat our dinner; our poor children are lost." "Here we are, O mother; here we are, O father," called the children, running and throwing themselves into their parents' arms. The mother embraced them, then took her soup ladle and whacked her husband, "Wham."

The next day, the father again took the children to the wilderness. This time, however, the daughter had no dates, and so she dropped popped barley instead. Again the father left them. He told them: "Do not worry. I will hang a jar in the tree. When it rattles (and it surely would rattle, for he had put a mouse in it), you will know that I'm coming." Then the father went home alone.

The boy and the girl waited and waited, but their father did not return, although the jar rattled. Then they tried to find their way home on their own. But the birds had eaten the popped barley and so no pathway was marked.

The boy and the girl continued the search. Finally, they came to a house where an old woman dwelled. She was blind in one eye and owned sheep and goats. The girl thought, "I will go up to the old woman and will milk her sheep as she milks them. But I will always stand on her blind side. That way she will not take note of me, nor see that I'm milking."

From day to day, the girl brought back milk for herself and her brother. The boy, however, kept protesting: "Take me on the milking; take me on the milking." Finally, the girl agreed to take him along. She warned him, however, in no case to speak. But when the boy saw the old woman, he laughed at the sight of her, and the witch caught both children.

The old woman put the children into earthenware jars and began to fatten them for eating. She gave honey to the one child and clarified butter to the other. The children ate well and got fat. The girl, however, saw the old woman's plot and so told her brother: "Hold up a piece of straw when the old woman asks to feel your finger. That way she won't eat us; she'll think we're still thin."

The old woman fed and fed them, but the children seemed to grow no fatter. Finally, in despair, she decided to eat them. At that luckless moment, a sparrow came to the children and sang: "When the old woman tells you to light the fire for the roasting, you must answer: 'My mother taught me to launder, my mother taught me to sweep, but my mother did not teach me to blow on a fire.' Then when the old woman begins to stoke the oven, push her into the flames." The girl did this and killed the old witch. (Various adventures are added at this point.)

The implications of the Hansel and Gretel tale, of course, are tragic, for while the virgin is capable of a near-perfect approximation of idealized motherhood, she is physically incapable of conceiving a child. On the other hand, the Moroccan genetrix cannot equal the selfless concern of the virgin because of her sexual awakening. The virgin is wanting at the physiological level, while the mother lacks a certain purity of spirit.

A virgin shows perceptiveness in addition to a nurturant tendency. That perceptiveness approaches wisdom, and yet because any virgin tends to lead a sheltered existence, it perforce is incomplete. The daughter speaks persuasively about the quinces and figs, for example, but her words save her father only incidentally, for the daughter is unaware of the true danger with which he is faced. In particular, she misjudges the Sultan, for she is unacquainted with royal preciousness and egotism. As importantly, however, she quickly guesses the deceitfulness of the Sultan's wives: she predicts their Eve-like desire for the first, sweetest taste of the fruit.

Inadequately shaped by social experience, the perspicacity of the virgin nonetheless develops through time. In the tale of Sersar Dehbun, it is the youngest, least experienced, and most trusting of the seven sisters who is spirited off and falls prey to the Sultan. Her six older sisters have better learned the value of suspicion.

Tale 14: Sersar Dehbun (Golden Bell)

There once was a man who had two sons and seven daughters. First his wife died and then he also. With that, the two sons left their sisters behind and went to work in the fields. As protection, the older son put seven doors and seven locks on the house, telling each sister that she should never go beyond hers. All obeyed except the youngest, Sersar Dehbun.

Sersar Dehbun went to the roof each day in order to brush her hair as her sisters cooked, swept, and hauled water. One day, a hunter spotted the virgin. Finding her beautiful, he went to the Sultan to report the prize that he had found. Forthwith, the ruler desired her as his wife and told the hunter to bring her to him.

The hunter returned to the brothers' house. He asked Sersar Dehbun for water, but the girl could not give it, for the door, as always, was locked. "Then lower the pail on your hair," the hunter commanded. She obeyed, and he pulled her down by the hair and carried her off.

The hunter and the virgin passed under a tree, and its leaves turned yellow. Then they slept under a second tree, and its leaves fell off. Close to the castle they passed under a third tree, and it began withering also. Finally, they reached the palace, where the Sultan took his new bride.

That same evening the older brother returned from his herding. He asked the six sisters where the youngest had gone. They replied that they had no inkling. Hoping to find her, the older brother sold his inheritance and went off, looking in all directions.

The brother searched along all possible paths. Finally, only one path was left to him. Passing under a tree, he saw that it was yellow. He asked the tree why, and it answered "because of Sersar Dehbun." Sleeping under another tree, he asked why no leaves were left on it, and it answered "Sersar Dehbun." Finding a third tree, he asked why it had withered, and it answered "because of Sersar Dehbun."

Following the trees, he soon reached the palace. There the brother asked for food and shelter and for three days was hosted as one should host any guest. During that time the Sultan's daughter came to trust him and so asked him to watch over her son.

One day, Sersar Dehbun saw her brother working. She sent him money but did not send for him to come to her, for no man entered the royal harem, upon penalty of death. Finally she told the guard to escort her brother when the Sultan was absent. She warned the guard not to tell the ruler or she would have her servants cut out his tongue.

The brother did not recognize his sister, for she was older and a princess and had already borne two children. When she revealed who she was, however, he asked her to return home. Sersar Dehbun responded that better could be done.

She put the care of her children into his hands. Then she had the Sultan make him prince over a nearby land. Finally, she asked her brother to kill her husband in order to obtain his kingdom. The brother refused to take part in the murder but agreed to seize control of the land.

Soon the brother married the daughter of the Sultan at his sister's behest. With the illness of the Sultan, he became ruling minister over the land. Finally, he became Sultan with the old

Sultan's death. In his turn, he made his younger brother minister. As for Sersar Dehbun, he sent her away from the palace, back to the country from which she had been spirited off.

MARRIAGE

The change from moral purity to its loss is largely foreordained for females, for the attainment of 'aqel makes probable its ultimate demise. The greater the 'aqel of the young virgin, the more tenaciously she will be courted. Hence the more likely will be her sexual awakening and spiritual temptation. Marriage, in fact, is often arranged for the folk virgin as a reward for a good and obedient life (tale 12).

Although Roudaniyin regard marriage as the major turning point in a woman's life, the down-swing, as the tales remind us, does not necessarily occur when marriage begins. Instead the fall is varyingly situated within an extended period in which the wife increases in social and sexual awareness. Likely to be timid in her new wifely role, the bride at first is scarcely married in mind. Instead she is often hesitant in her social dealings, restrained in her sexual relations, and economically cautious. It requires time, say Roudaniyin, for many brides to develop a callous self-servingness.

The physical changes that Roudaniyin associate with sexual experience in women are also believed to develop with time. Informants speak of a facial shift from roundness to gauntness and a change in skin tone from pinkness to black. The virgin's cheeks are said to be full; the married woman's become hollow. The virgin is said to exhibit a pink hue under her eyes while the married woman shows darkness. Sersar Dehbun (tale 14) not only changes in character by virtue of her marriage, becoming mercenary and demanding, she also evinces a marked change in appearance, one that is so total that her own brother does not recognize her, despite her life of comfort and ease.

These beliefs about physiognomy, of course, help rationalize the desire for the more attractive state called virginity. Virgins are superordinately attractive to Taroudannt's men. This is admitted by men and is perceived to be a gnawing reality by women. No man interviewed lauded the *hejjala* (nonvirgin) over the virgin as bride. No woman felt that sexual experience and the greater finesse, fervor, and understanding that might proceed from it provided adequate compensation for the loss of virginity. Indeed, sexual finesse and fervor are often associated with prostitutes and are therefore to be shunned. Instead, some husbands hoped for limited responsiveness; they expected their wives to evince shame to such a degree that they could not tell whether intercourse had caused pain or pleasure. The response that they encouraged approximates the reticence of the virginal bride.

Beliefs about the lesser attractiveness of women who have undergone defloration have important psychological effects on those women. Most broadly they engender an ambivalence about how married womanhood is viewed. In many ways, it is clear that marriage brings the Moroccan married woman a marked rise in prestige, a fact in which she can find considerable delight. She suddenly is invited to join other women at festivities; she is sought out by older women for help and companionship; she discovers a new forum for her opinions and thoughts. A new array of economic resources passes through her hands. But at the same moment that a fresh social world is opened, the door to the old world closes sharply. Part of her feeling of exile is rooted in the perception of imminent physiological loss: "A woman is like an apricot," says one proverb, "eighteen days and she is out of season." Part results from her actual social exile: a bride and her virginal friends no longer fraternize after the wedding. She has sat with them in her bridal chamber on the evening before the consummation and has entertained them on the third day of the wedding week, but both occasions are farewells of a kind. Should the involvement continue, husband and mother-in-law will punish and scold. Condemnation will be harsh. For many young brides, the changeover is a hard one, but one that can scarcely be resisted. As in other things, the route from virginity to adulthood is made irreversible, which breeds its sadness among those women.

PREGNANCY

Pregnancy occupies a unique place in the period after defloration. Unlike other stages of a woman's adulthood, it constitutes a moral respite of a sort. Ruled by a morally pure being whose desires are made known as urgent demands, the pregnant woman takes on her own sort of purity. Allah forgives the sins that she incurs during pregnancy, for example, because they are no longer seen as volitional but rather are felt to be products of the mother-to-be's discomfort. At least a portion of those sins incurred before pregnancy are also discounted in the light of her pain.

The bestowing of grace seems to occur in these cases because the woman is felt temporarily to regain the positive social responsiveness associated with girlhood and virginity. Unlike the non-pregnant, sexually aware woman, whose egotism is said to lead to a heightened interest in material objects and sex, the mother-to-be realigns her priorities, making her child her primary focus. Or rather, the fetus establishes itself as a primary force impinging upon the mother-to-be's needs. What the fetus desires, the mother also desires; when the mother is denied, the fetus reacts. When the fetus craves food, for example, the pregnant woman also craves it; and when the mother's cravings are ignored, the mother scratches, and her child is disfigured in the area of the scratch.

As a consequence of this forced maternal involvement, the mother-to-be is felt likely to exhibit a lessened concern with her own personal well-being. In the following tale, a pregnant woman reacts bravely in the face of a threat which others flee coweringly. Her trust leads her, her child, and her husband to gain financial rewards.

Tale 15: The Talking Roof

A houseowner rented one of his houses over and over. People rented it in the daytime, and that same evening they left. They complained that the roof spoke. "I want to fall; I want to fall," it said. With that, people became frightened and quickly moved out.

One day a poor man came and begged for free lodging. The houseowner put him into the house with the talking roof, for as always, it was empty. The man thankfully entered, bringing his wife, who was near giving birth.

Later that day, while her husband was gone, the wife went into labor. And while she was in labor, the roof spoke: "I want to fall; I want to fall." "Just fall, O my brother," she answered, for she was caught up in pain. With that it fell, dropping all manner of silver.

The woman gave birth to her baby, all the while leaving the silver untouched. Then some time after the birth, she approached it. "In the name of God," she said in order to ward off the spirits that had entered into it over the years. Then she took a goatskin and gathered up the silver that had dropped.

When her husband returned, the woman described how the roof had talked, how she had answered, and how much had fallen. Her husband believed her and took some of the silver to buy a sacrifice for their new child. He also bought food and utensils. As to the house, he rented it from its owner. Thereafter, the couple lacked nothing, for they carefully spent the money that she had found.

While the grace that is provided to women through pregnancy is real according to the schema, that grace perforce is also short-lived, for it is the by-product of a forced psychological state. The pregnant woman is selfless not through free will but rather through the demands of the parasitic being within her. Once delivered of her child, the mother is believed to return to previous ways. The degeneracy that many tales impute to mothers once delivery and breastfeeding have been completed demonstrates the notion of the fleeting impact of pregnancy. Compare, for example, the response of the woman of Ergita (tale 24), still carrying her child on her back when she finds a silver cache, to the response of the still-pregnant woman of the previous tale.

OLD AGE

As men turn away from aging, experienced nonvirgins, these women are felt to engage in a strategic struggle for survival by using weapons of other kinds. With their seductiveness largely gone, slyness and deceit are the primary options left to them, and they are seen as likely to use these to establish their security and, beyond that, to amass power. The older woman, or 'aguz, for example, uses her experience in sexual matters in order to help others pursue their illicit sexual desires. She searches out male clients much as she does female clients and works at reprehensible tasks, shamelessly and mercenarily. Most often she dupes men, but she also shows little loyalty to women, betraying them quite as easily for an acceptable price.

Tale 16: The Gray Hair
A man always divorced and remarried. Finding a woman who seemed to fulfill all his wishes, he promised her on the wedding night: "Until gray shows at your temples, I will not marry again." Soon afterward, however, the husband felt the urge to take a new wife. So he went to mwa 'aguz in order to find out how he might extricate himself from his vow.

Said *mwa 'aguz:* "Your wife will never get gray, for her life is too easy. So make it more difficult. Tell her that you are sick and that you have gone to a religious curer or *taleb.* Tell her, too, that he advised you to eat only from clay pots (not aluminum or copper). Then buy clay pots and bring home green kindling. Soon you will have what you desire."

That same day the wife began to cook in the first clay pot. She pushed the green wood under the pot, but of course, could not light it. Pushing more and more wood under it in order to stoke the fire, she finally broke the clay. Porridge poured all over. This happened with the second pot and more times, until a gray hair emerged.

Some days later, the husband sat down to his dinner. He said to his wife, "Do you remember our vow? It is over, for there is a gray hair at your temple." His wife responded with despair and dissatisfaction: "With this kind of living, even young boys go gray." So perceptive were her words that her husband had a change of heart. He did not divorce her, nor did he take a second wife.

Shamefully inappropriate to Moroccans is the occasional unfettered sexuality of old women. No longer able to bear children and seen as incapable of pleasing men because of waning attractiveness (it is said that the eye of covetousness has passed over them), older women have a sexuality that they should no longer display. And yet aging women are felt to have difficulty in showing good sense and propriety, so powerful are their sexual propensities and needs.

Tale 17: The Night Grinding

There once was a man, his wife, and his mother, the last being an old woman. One day a stranger came to their door, asking for a place to stay for the night. The household head let him in and left him to sleep in the kitchen. And in those days, women ground barley and *argan* (oil) seeds in the night. That night the mother ground them not in the vestibule but rather in the kitchen. Later she sang:

Happiness, O my mother,
Light has entered my room;
The lovely acts of this guest
Have reminded me of what was forgotten.

She sang this verse until sunrise.

These beliefs about older women's sexual propensities deeply affect Moroccans' attitudes about marriage in later life. Even when the bride-to-be requires the financial support that her new husband provides, onlookers inevitably impute sexual motivations to her desire for union. Derision, for example, was the local response when the sixtyish mother of one of the city's more respected citizens took an elderly *faqir* (religious devotee) as her spouse. "She needs someone to warm her mat," neighbors said jokingly. The image of depravity lasted through the years.

WOMEN AND SAINTHOOD

How, then, can a woman avoid the moral pitfalls generated through her sexuality? The answer is obvious at one level and is clearly provided in the few Taroudannt folktales which concern Moroccan women as saints. The truly judicious and saintly female can avoid the fate of her sex by shunning defloration and marriage. This is the message that the rather sparse tale of Lalla Miriam Ali communicates.

Tale 18: Lalla Miriam Ali

There was a virgin who grazed her father's sheep each day. She would graze them until nightfall and then would wash ritually, change her garments, and pray. One day, her father said that she should marry, but she refused, saying that she wished to remain chaste. After she died, two springs were found near her home and were attributed to her: one occurred where water fell from her ritual washings; the other stream sprang up one day in order to quench the saint's thirst.

A second alternative is provided for those few saintly heroines who are already sexually awakened but who hold off or temporarily roll back the course of female frailty through certain superhuman acts. This kind of woman is best sustained in her sainthood through supernatural intervention: she is taken directly to heaven before she can slide back.

Tale 19: The Prostitute Saint

Once there were two sisters, one of them married with children, the other an unmarried prostitute. The two lived in their father's house, the first as a dutiful housekeeper while the second went out soliciting. One day their neighbor needed some charcoal and came to the house. Pregnant, she smelled a chicken cooking on the fire and desired a taste of it. The dutiful wife responded, giving her a smidgin of broth.

The chicken, however, haunted the pregnant woman's thoughts, and so she returned asking for a bit of the charcoal. The dutiful wife gave her the coals but offered no more of the broth. A third, a fourth, and up to a tenth time, the woman returned for some coals, but by then the chicken and the broth had been hidden. Finally, unsatisfied, the woman lowered herself in front of the cook's door and uncontrollably cried.

At that moment, the prostitute passed by. She asked her neighbor why she was weeping. The woman answered that she had gone to the dutiful wife ten times because of the chicken but had received none of the meat.

With that, the prostitute went to her sister. She asked for some chicken, but the sister responded: "Men always give you food. Here I have finally managed to buy a chicken for my children. You will get none of it." Again the prostitute asked her and again the sister refused. Finally, the prostitute said that she would buy the chicken and the broth, giving half the house, her share of the inheritance. The dutiful wife gleefully accepted. The prostitute then fed her neighbor and walked off.

The next morning, the dutiful sister and her husband woke early. They called to the prostitute, for they were eager to be rid of her. Receiving no answer, they entered her room. There they found a pair of silver scissors, the scissors with which the angels had cut and sewn her funerary garments. Body and garments, however, were already gone.

The immediate transfer of the saintly woman to the afterlife says much about how female holiness is viewed. In particular, it serves as a potent commentary upon the degree to which a sexually experienced woman is believed to be capable of maintaining her saintliness. The male saint achieves holiness and then proceeds to live it: its attainment is but a first step in a continuingly devout human life. The female saint, by contrast, must be shielded from herself by death if need be, or she will inevitably slide back into a sinful life.

Female sainthood and female development then stand essentially at odds, a tension which perhaps partially explains why there are so few female saints in Morocco and why their lives are so little elaborated in believers' minds. In Taroudannt, there is Lalla Mimuna, the date palm; there is Lalla Mbaraka, a stone wrapped in cloth; and there is Lalla Soliha, the only one of the three that is remembered as a woman but significantly one whose history has been lost. All are imperfectly anthropomorphized and scarcely sexual. Nor can they easily be. The female saint does best either to fixate her development at a pregenital stage, or to divorce herself from human society. In both cases, her behavior, when projected on a grand scale, bodes ill for humankind. In the end, even if a girl should desire to travel the saintly route, kinfolk and neighbors are apt to discourage her. They push her out of the Golden Age and away from her saintly proclivities, opting instead to help satisfy society's more immediate procreative needs. If one

believes the schema, the choice is likely to bring on the fall; as
Roudaniyin might say helplessly, if sadly, it can scarcely be
avoided.

MOTHERS AND DAUGHTERS

The belief that older women are likely to lead younger women
into sin accords with the Taroudannt stance that brides should be
sought far off. "Farm nearby; marry far" says one Roudaniy
proverb, for the family of the groom particularly distrusts the older
women of the bride's family. Those women are felt to breed
discontent, encourage unreasonable demands, and provide a
refuge for unhappy brides. When a husband or a mother-in-law
scolds or punishes, the bride is likely to recall her mother's (and
perhaps also her father's) every-ready protection, pack up, and
walk off. The husband then must win her back or find a new wife.

Let us consider the case of the bride Rabi'a and her mother
Tamu, for the judgment rendered in the court case concerning her
especially gives voice to these fears. The widow Tamu, hard-
working, temperate, and upstanding, gave her daughter Rabi'a in
marriage to an emigrant worker, son of a woman living in the
adjoining block. Although the young male worker was known to
be frivolous, Tamu nonetheless deemed the marriage advantageous, for she reasoned that young men are often light-headed
but also often reform. Moreover, workers in Belgium receive a
considerable wage and are absent from the home all but several
weeks a year, the times of their vacations. How trying, then, could
the young husband be?

As the marriage developed, the answer became apparent.
Rabi'a's husband proved difficult even from afar, for he sent
insufficient money for his bride's support, even though Rabi'a was

pregnant. And worse, the little money that was sent never reached his wife, for it was quickly seized by an unsympathetic mother-in-law, who exercised her right to supervise the family finances with an uncompromising hand. Rabi'a submitted to this control during the first few months, but complained bitterly and increasingly during each of her mother's frequent visits.

Tamu, in her turn, provided advice. Her first counsel was patience, but gradually the mother also showed anger and supported desertion as a recourse should matters get worse. Rabi'a immediately seized that alternative during her next dispute with her mother-in-law. With the lightened heart, she walked out of the house vowing never to return.

Tamu, however, soon realized the danger, for the desertion was ill-timed: there was no husband present to coax her daughter back. So she ordered Rabi'a quickly to return to the mother-in-law's house. There the girl banged on the door while neighbors gathered, but the old woman would not let her in.

Eventually, Tamu sued for a court order to provide her daughter with reentry into her marital home, noting the mother-in-law's treachery and stinginess throughout the affair. The mother-in-law, for her part, stated that the bride had forfeited her rights, for she had deserted her husband. She said that the girl's evil inclinations, along with her mother's poisonous influence, had impelled her to misdeeds.

Faced with this disparity of positions and accounts, the judge followed his own inclinations. Rabi'a was to return to her husband's house, for she carried the family's heir in her womb. The bride's mother, however, was debarred from seeing her daughter during the subsequent six months (the duration of the pregnancy) and thereafter was to limit her visits. The judge posed the last two conditions because he agreed with the mother-in-law in her scathing criticism of Tamu: the mother was a evil influence who encouraged her daughter's discontent.

It must be stressed that isolation from the mother, and from women like her, is not merely viewed as a way to reduce a bride's supportive ranks. It also prevents techniques and practices which are detrimental to the groom from reaching the girl's consciousness. The case of the bride Ftoma provides an apt illustration. Married illegally at the age of thirteen, Ftoma had just recently begun menstruating prior to the wedding, a fact into which her mother read danger, for it spelled the possibility of a quick pregnancy. Pregnancy, in turn, meant Ftoma's likely ensconcement, for the birth of children brings a degree of marital stability, whether wives want it or not. Ftoma's mother, however, in no way wanted that stability during those early months, for her son-in-law was young and frivolous, a youth who might later provide severe problems for his bride should he remain childish. So the mother acted secretly. On the wedding night she had an older woman steal the bowl in which henna and sweet-smelling spices were mixed for the bride's hair. Then she turned the bowl over onto itself, "extinguishing it," and hid it away in her kitchen in that reversed position. In that way, the girls' womb was magically closed, and time was provided for signs to appear as to whether or not the marriage was auspicious.

It is telling in this case that Ftoma did not know of the sorcery that her mother had worked on her behalf. Indeed, the mother stated adamantly that she should not know, for the girl would inevitably protest. A mother, said Ftoma's mother, could view her daughter's long-range future, with the hindsight of a woman who had endured many disappointments and hardships. A newly married daughter could not look beyond her present joys, particularly the new status of wife and the even greater status of mother. Ftoma's mother reasoned that no bride could put off the tasting of those benefits, whatever the risk.

In a society like Morocco, in which reproduction is one main goal of marriage, the mother's action emerges as at once antisocial, unnatural, and irreligious. Contraception, like abortion, is prohibited in Islam, and yet the mother leads her daughter into committing that sin. She does it, Moroccans would say, out of a certain magnanimity, but also because she, like many older women, cannot see beyond a world of narrowly defined female priorities; through actions like hers, the interests of the community of the faithful and the will of Allah are said to be subordinated to women's "base" desires and instincts.

Chapter Five
FROM BOY TO MAN

The boy of ten is like a peeled cucumber.
The man of twenty makes friendships with
    fools.
The man of thirty (is like the) flower of the
    garden.
The man of forty is in his prime.

Palestinian proverb
(Granqvist 1931: 37)

GOALLESSNESS

"The kitchen has fallen in upon us," say Moroccan men and women good-naturedly when a girl child is born. The phrase conveys both the negative and positive feelings associated with the event. The kitchen implies materiality and limitedness in scope rather than a blossoming religiosity and potentiality. It has "fallen in" says that the female component is overweighted, although it might be to the good, as the tale of the talking roof (tale 15) indicates. And yet the additional person belongs to the household's core, the food-producing, life-sustaining quarter, and so the new daughter's contribution must be seen as positive in the sense that it is located within a vital sphere. By contrast, no such standard phrase greets the birth of a son, nor can it, for sons can make many or few social contributions, and there is much doubt as to whether a son's efforts will heighten good living within the household's bounds.

Thus the birth of a girl child tends to be ushered in with a degree of quiet assurance. There is happiness among the women. After all, girls help in the home: a little girl at the age of five might run errands to the local shopkeepers; at age seven she likely will begin sweeping the rooms; at ten she will launder; and at twelve, she is deemed capable of hauling water, making bread, and cooking whole meals. Her housekeeping repertoire is essentially complete at that age. Similarly, maternal tasks enter into a young girl's worktime and playtime. At three, the child Su'ad took an old cloth and tied an old oil bottle on her back with it. At five, she moved on to the larger size and softer feel of a sitting-room cushion; she lumbered beneath it but nonetheless persevered, her originality provoking laughter and rewarding comments from neighbors and kin. At age six, she graduated to carrying her baby brother on her back. With a towel wrapped around herself and the baby, Su'ad swayed sideways in rhythm, much as her mother would. Her contribution provided hours of relief and release for her mother, who again was pregnant.

And if Su'ad was helpful to her mother, so was her fourteen-year-old sister. Apart from providing household help, that girl listened to her mother's complaints about men with abiding sympathy. The two females, the one a woman, the other almost so, supported one another in their dealings with men.

Women's lot is harder if families are without daughters—
women's emotional companions, household aides, and political
compatriots. Women recognize these advantages and generally
state a preference for a female firstborn not only as they talk about
this possibility during pregnancy but also as they talk wistfully
about their futures before marriage. That preference, however,
remains voiced predominantly within the world of girls and
women, for men initially hope for the birth of a male.

While men display their inclination for firstborn sons, they also
recognize the importance of having daughters for women. Hence
they generally do not hope for sons only, for they know that a
wife's lot will then be immeasurably harder and that they, the
husbands, will perforce suffer along. The frequent lamentations of
one well-to-do shopkeeper underscore this point: he had to hire a
full-time maid to help his wife, who had dutifully borne him six
sons. Theoretically the ideal in a society that is said to prefer male
offspring, those many sons were in no way viewed by kinfolk or
neighbors as an advantage.

Men's, as well as women's, appreciation of daughters is
reflected in proverbs from the region and more general Islamic
traditions. "He whose first child is one with a vulva was gladdened
by God," says one Islamic tradition that is cited by Moroccans.
Similarly, in many regions of Morocco, the bearing of many
daughters by the populace is taken to be an omen of future
prosperity (Westermarck 1930: 89); good feelings will characterize the year.

However helpful daughters are felt to be and however much
women desire female offspring, it is nonetheless true that the birth
of a son occasions a more overt, more extroverted response.
There are public expressions of happiness on the part of women
in the household: the women *zgharet*—trill loudly and joyously—
at the moment of birth, with the sound carrying to far-off houses.

No trills accompany the birth of a daughter. Traditionally, there were gunshots, again only for boys. At present, there still tend to be heartier congratulations from outside the family, and fathers sometimes expend greater amounts of money for entertainment during the several days that culminate with the *subu'*, or seventh day of sacrifice and naming. And yet there is also the shadow of a greater uncertainty which seems to emerge despite or through that increased action and display, for it is expected that the male will be quixotic as a child, willful as an adolescent, and often disconcertingly independent as an adult. While the female child carries with her a degree of release and relief for the mother, the male child carries with him an ongoing uncertainty. These recurrent doubts occur among fathers as well as mothers: while fathers do not profit from their daughters' help to the degree that mothers do, they certainly expect to suffer through the difficulties that sons cause.

One can readily intuit the strain associated with the male child from the congratulatory phrases that meet the occasion of his birth. "Blessings to the bachelor," say the guests and visitors, thereby calling attention to that stage prior to marriage when males prove most frustrating to their parents. "Blessings to the virgin (ready for marriage)," one announces for the girl child, the focus there being upon the period when girls more nearly exhibit good sense.

The heightened level of anxiety that emerges with respect to sons on this and other occasions has an economic association. A son should ideally come to be the mainstay of his family, and yet his propensities, it is felt, militate against this happening at every early stage. A daughter, by contrast, is expected to make no economic contribution, and so causes no worry to her parents on that count. Indeed, she threatens chiefly in one way: the family's honor is linked to her virginity. Thus family efforts are narrowly defined in the case of a daughter: they focus upon the task of quickly marrying her off. Thereafter anxiety levels decrease. Indeed, a daughter thereafter is perceived as providing her parents with a relatively certain source of support, generally emotional but sometimes also financial.

Thus parents typically expect that daughters, not sons, will support them in times of trouble. A daughter is termed "the key of the house" (Westermarck 1930: 89), in that she looks after it and its owners. By extension, a daughter is also said to mourn her parents upon the latters' deaths: "He who has no daughters, the people will not know when he died" (Westermarck 1930: 89), say Dukkala Moroccans as well as Roudaniyin. A girl child is believed to exhibit an innate attachment to her parents: she is thought to be incapable of negating her filial devotion, much as she is felt to be incapable of rising above her cravings for sex in her awakened years.

Initial commentaries about boys' births have underlying negative connotations because negative motivations are imputed to boys during their childhood years. Egotistical spontaneity is expected of the male child from his earliest days. His motivation (xaṭer) is said to be narrow (diyyeq). Mothers thus are apt to expect that their small sons will be quick to cry for food; they expect that their sons might become angered if not immediately appeased. Indeed, small boys are said to cry often without reason, merely craving attention. Significantly, women accept these reactions good-naturedly when they occur, for they are deemed somewhat expectable from the male sex. Most often women respond with smiling or laughter: "Look, he is upset" is a typical mother's comment. It can be taken to be synomonous with "Look, he is demonstrating that he is male."

Impassioned spontaneity is expected from the male child even while he is still in the womb. Already as a fetus the male is believed to be a bundle of energy that is predisposed to movement. The male fetus is believed to flit from side to side in the abdomen, nervously covering his ground. Similarly, the milk of a still-pregnant mother is said to mix completely with water if she is to bear a male child. Girls, by contrast, are felt to be more controlled and more purposive even in the womb. They are believed to sit contentedly, low in the abdomen. The breast fluids of their mothers are believed to remain quietly atop water. Indeed, some sage-like old women assert that they can predict the maleness or femaleness of a child from such signs.

The putative calmness of girls and effusiveness of boys as they pass through the fetal and infant stages are felt to be consistent with the behavior that the two sexes show in their later years. The Taroudannt version of the Hansel and Gretel tale reveals this consistency in its male and female characterizations. In the Taroudannt tale, Hansel acts with a self-centered lack of concern for his sister. He cannot and will not remain silent while the witch is near the house, his propensity for motion and expression sealing both children's doom. Gretel, by contrast, calmly takes charge after the desertion, and works efficaciously for both children's well-being. She emerges as forthright and heavy *(tqila),* say Roudaniyin, while her brother emerges as undependable and light *(xfif).*

The Taroudannt version of the Hansel and Gretel tale nicely contrasts with the Grimm version in terms of its messages about boyhood and girlhood. Grimm's Hansel, the same age or somewhat older than his sister, leads and comforts his sister, who is instinctively afraid. "Don't worry," says Grimm's Hansel before he gathers the pebbles that he will strew on the path in order to lead both children home. "Don't weep," he again counsels before he strews the crumbs that the birds will later eat from the roadside. In the Grimm version, it is Hansel who cleverly holds out the bone so that the witch will think that his finger has not fattened. In the Moroccan version, Gretel holds up the straw in order to misguide the witch. Grimm's Hansel is active and independent, while Taroudannt's Hansel remains irresponsible and wholly dependent upon women.

CIRCUMCISION

There is one life crisis imposed upon boys during their rather
spontaneous childhood: circumcision. Through his circumcision,
which generally takes place between the ages of 2 and 8 years,
the boy child is forcibly prepared for his subsequent sexual life, for
as Roudaniyin affirm, he cannot become a proper Muslim social-
sexual being without it. Circumcision is a religious obligation, and
also constitutes an aesthetic expectation: no proper Muslim
woman, they affirm, should accept a man without that validating
mark.

Circumcision constitutes a physical and emotional trauma for
any Taroudannt boy child. Torn from his female relatives, who
must not be present at the operation, carried by his male kin who
will then forcibly restrain him, cut by a male nurse or a barber
whom he has never before met, even the first child in the group
finds the experience agonizing in numerous ways, Roudaniyin are
wont to say, and this is even more true for the later ones who have
heard the screams of the ones that went before them.

And yet adults also view the trauma as being ephemeral. Boys,
for example, are adjudged to remain characterologically the same
through and after it. A boy should be aware at the moment of the
circumcision: hence he should in no case be too young (Jewish
circumcision, which occurs soon after birth, is therefore considered to be reprehensible), and should not be anaesthetized. And
yet that awareness is sought predominantly so that he will remember the experience in later life rather than use it as a basis for
immediate introspection.

The comments of mothers reflect their belief that the circumcision experience does not assume cognitive weight at the boys'
rather young age. Fatima dressed her three-year-old son for the
operation, wistfully adorning him with the traditional white robe
and a yellow and white headband, and then commented sadly
upon his innocently beautiful appearance. "Look, he is pleased;

he does not know what awaits him," she added to the other
women, directly in front of the still smiling child. Fatima felt that
the boy could not foresee the imminent danger, nor would he
guess at its full effect even upon hearing her foreboding. And if the
boy child cannot properly ponder the experience before its occurrence, he cannot properly appreciate it immediately afterward, it is
believed. Many mothers threaten circumcision as a way of con-
trolling their boys, much as they might threaten a pinch or a slap.
Most feel that the memory has little social, religious, or psychological meaning; the boy remembers only the gross outlines of pain.

   Circumcision thus is an anticipatory act in that it fulfills a social
and religious obligation which the male child will truly understand
only later in life. It is also anticipatory in the sexual sense. Circumcision does not make a boy sexual or awaken his sexuality, as
defloration does for women. Rather it gives the boy child a proper
physical shape in preparation for the moment when his sexual
desires come to be actualized, which can occur at any time.

SEXUAL AWAKENING

The self-centered spontaneity that the male infant and child
exhibits, it is believed, does not diminish as he moves into adolescence. Instead the youth merely channels his cravings more
strategically as he becomes worldly wise. More clever and more
aware, he no longer needs mother or sister to intercede for him as
he seeks to satisfy his desires. Instead he strikes out on his own,
using whomever he meets in order to fulfill them. In many
Taroudannt tales (e.g., tales 13, 14) a girl is lured from her house,
but in none is she motivated to move out spontaneously. By
contrast, only one boy, Hansel, is lured away from his household,
while several are spontaneously driven to forsake their homes.

Primary among the desires that force the male adolescent out into the world is his sexual craving, which, like all his other drives, takes the form of a spontaneous need. The country youth who is continually drawn to the city for sex, the city boy who runs after whatever girl he fancies, are both expressing what is felt to be their inescapable adolescent sexuality, and both men and women accept this behavior as inevitable. Thus Taroudannt mothers generally talk of their sons' forays to local prostitutes without the horror that Western mothers might exhibit. They appear little concerned with their sons' seeming lack of discernment, for a lack of discernment is expectable at this stage. Rather whatever fears they might express focus upon women—upon loose female neighbors or known prostitutes who through their wiliness might arrest the social and spiritual development of those youths.

Given the image of sexually knowledgeable women, there is logic to these maternal fears. The adult woman is felt to possess a powerful sexuality, and the young boy is believed to be most able to match it. These older women, however, can hardly rely upon youths to maintain their sexual interest, for circumstances gradually push many adolescents into a more sober adulthood. A prostitute thus must use supernatural devices in order to prolong the young male's sexual desire for her. She takes the cloth with which the man has wiped off his semen and burns it as incense. She dips a cloth into the blood of someone who has died without warning, unaware, and wears it in a pouch around her neck. Through the smell of the burned cloth or the pouch, the male finds that his freedom is suddenly lost.

The prostitute seeks to arrest the sexual development of the young man in order to satisfy her sexual desires. In this sense, she is socially disruptive. In seeking to fulfill his own sexual urges, however, the male adolescent is also neglectful of societal needs. Driven by sex, he tries in underhanded ways to make women's acquaintance. He annoys, seduces, and pesters, and is adamantly aggressive. Indeed, social order would crumble under the weight of his egotism except for the fact that he gets his way only rarely because of the crudeness of his techniques.

The tale of Aisha, the carpenter's daughter, presents the bold sexuality and the clumsiness of the male youth in full measure. In that tale, the son of the Sultan transgresses many of Morocco's fundamental values, among them those involving the sacredness of hospitality, the protection of female purity, and the privacy of home life, so strong are his sexual tendencies. Indeed, in his attempt to win over the virgin, he betrays even his most essential characteristic, his masculine identity.

Tale 20: Aisha, the Carpenter's Daughter

There once was a man who had three daughters, the oldest being Aisha. His family lived across the street from the Sultan. Sometimes Aisha would go up to her roof in order to wash her hair, and the Sultan's son would see her. Desiring her, the Sultan's son decided to seduce her while Aisha's father was on pilgrimage. He dressed like a woman and went to visit the girl.

Taking a potful of food, the Sultan's son knocked and asked if she were ailing. Aisha let in the "woman" who evinced such concern and sympathy, accepted the food, and the four "females"—Aisha, her two sisters, and the Sultan's son—sat down to sup. But Aisha did not eat, for she feared deception. Instead she watched cautiously. After her two sisters ate, they keeled over unconscious. Aisha, however, remained vigilant, so that the son of the Sultan had no sway over her. Eventually he fled.

The next day, Aisha went to the roof and saw the Sultan's son studying. He called to her, "Good morning." She answered with an insult: "You have dripped soup on your shirt." "Count the number of leaves on that basil plant," said he, attempting to begin a conversation. "Count the number of lines in your book," she answered, as if to say "continue your work."

Some months later, Aisha's father returned from the pilgrimage. Again the son of the Sultan approached her. "Your father will come to me crying and laughing," he said tauntingly, for so a father appears when he gives his daughter in marriage. Aisha sent her father to him crying from onions and yet laughing about the meaninglessness of his tears.

The next week, the youth asked where Aisha's mother and father had gone. She responded, "My father is growing water with water," meaning he was watering watermelon. "My mother went to wake a soul from a soul," meaning she was serving as a midwife. Again the youth did not understand.

Finally, the son of the Sultan determined to secure his vengeance. He went to Aisha's father and asked for her in marriage. His goal was to leave his bride buried in a well eternally as punishment for the annoyance that she had caused. But Aisha quickly dug a tunnel from the well to her house after overhearing his plan.

The couple married, and each day the son of the Sultan lowered a piece of bread to his bride in the well, for he gave her only bread to eat. Each day, as the bread came, she asked him to acknowledge her victory over him. He always responded, however, that he, the male, had won in their match.

Finally, Aisha heard that her husband planned to embark on a voyage. She left just ahead of him. When he arrived in that far land, he heard people say that a beautiful young virgin was newly arrived in the town. The son of the Sultan sought her out, found her plump and beautiful, and slept with her. She asked only his ring in payment for the night.

Almost a year later, the son of the Sultan again decided to travel, and Aisha went before him into the second land. There, people raved of a newly arrived, beautiful young woman to the Sultan's son. He visited and slept with her. Rejecting his money, she asked only for the strap to his bag.

Finally, the Sultan's son traveled to a third land. In the third land he slept with a lovely round woman. She also asked for the strap of his bag in the place of money for the night.

And from the three matings, three children were born: Suriya, Sur, and Nur, so named after the lands in which they were conceived. In her house near the well, Aisha raised and cared for them.

After some years, the Sultan decided that his son should remarry. On the wedding night, the new bride sat in her bridal room awaiting her groom. At that point, Aisha sent over her three sons, telling them to knock over belongings and to bother the guests. Hearing the commotion, the son of the Sultan came out to stop them. He captured the children, who then showed him the ring and the straps.

The Sultan's son asked them to identify their mother. Hearing that it was Aisha, he returned to the well. He found her at the bottom, so plump and beautiful that she barely could fit in that small space. He also found a roomful of bread in her house, for she had touched none of the food that he had provided for her.

With that, the son of the Sultan called down the well and asked Aisha to join him properly as his wife. Aisha responded: "Who, then, has won the contest, the man or the woman?" "The woman," he answered. He then moved Aisha out of the well into his house and sent the bride-to-be home.

As the tale of Aisha indicates, the virgin is innately responsible and so must be forced into sexual awareness; the male youth is innately sexual and so must be forced into a socially responsible state. Given this model of the male adolescent's tendencies, the impetus for marriage necessarily arises through other than the boy's efforts. Similarly, acceptance must necessarily come from other than the female.

It is thus logical that the parents of a bachelor initiate and carry through the complex search for a suitable bride. This is the Moroccan custom. The woman Fatima, for example, acted acceptably when she called to her son and announced that it was time that he take a wife. By extension, her intense involvement in the search, during which she systematically examined all neighboring virgins who were potential spouses, was regarded as careful, dutiful, and vigilant by all. Fatima visited friends and neighbors who had daughters and noted the traits of the girls who passed by and served her. She watched the demeanor and relative comeliness of the nearly-naked virgins in the bath house as they washed. She even entered into strangers' homes on pretext: she knocked at doors and asked for directions or water and noted the behavior of the girls who hovered in the background inside. Fatima was persistent, neighbors said, and they smiled as they thought of it. She was excessive, but her search bore its fruit. After months of pursuit, she finally saw a virgin who totally pleased her. Not so striking that her son might be too taken with his wife, not so worldly that the bride would feel longings to travel or socialize, Fatima's choice was a country girl who knew the value of work. For his part, Fatima's son was quite taken with his mother's efforts and openly acknowledged the qualities of the girl that his mother had found.

The need for this kind of parental surveillance is apparent in those tales which describe how a bachelor selects a bride if left to his own devices. In these mythic cases, the male neglects the subtler, more socially useful virtues of women and blindly pursues ephemeral, inessential attributes. In fact, the adolescent often proceeds along his course unrealistically, his physiological drives are so great. In one folktale, for example, a male suitor asks a go-between to find a fiancée "with two" (sets of genitalia), a not-so-oblique reference to his need for a woman who is more than a woman. More clever and astute, the go-between turns his request to her own and her client's advantage.

Tale 21: The Bride with Two

There once was a man who wanted a wife with two. So he went to *mwa 'aguz* in order to see whom she could find for him. "There are such girls," she answered. "I will bring you one."

Mwa 'aguz went to a mother whose daughter was ready for marriage. She told her that someone wanted to affiance her daughter, but that he wanted a virgin with two. The mother replied that her daughter had only one and that, in fact, no females with two existed. *Mwa 'aguz* answered that one was all that the new bride would need.

Mwa 'aguz brought the man to visit his bride-to-be. While the man stood unbeknown to the girl in the courtyard, the old woman told the girl to prepare herself for prayer on the landing. As the girl bent toward the well in order to draw water for the ritual washing, *mwa 'aguz* said to the suitor, "See the one that she has behind" (for undergarments are not worn in prayer). Then, as the girl stood up to pray, *mwa 'aguz* offered, "See the one that she has in front." The man was convinced and took the girl as his bride.

The wedding week passed smoothly, for *mwa 'aguz* cautioned that the bride could use only the front one in those early days. Before the second could be used, the first had to undergo a ritual washing. Then on that day of the washing, *mwa 'aguz* took a sparrow whose wings had been partially defeathered: she put it into a jar and gave it to the bride, who left it with her husband. The bride cautioned him not to peak inside or to let others see the second while she was away.

The husband, however, was curious as to how the second looked. So he opened the jar, loosing the sparrow. "Here is your penis," the man called frantically to the escaped bird, as he raised his overgarment. But the sparrow was long gone.

Mwa 'aguz was secretly watching, and quickly carried the good news to the bath, telling the bride to return home. When the bride entered, she asked her husband for her second one. But the husband answered: "Enough. One is enough. It is all that I want." His wife, of course, acquiesced in his demand.

FIRST STEPS TOWARD WISDOM

The marriage of the male adolescent might be seen as a necessary first step in a man's halting progress toward wisdom. By no means, however, does it provide a sufficient condition for wisdom to be attained. The young male can divorce his new wife essentially at will. He can annoy her through a vengeful urge. He can wander off, leaving her hungry and penniless with only the courts as a rather ineffectual, ultimate recourse for her in her need. In sum, he can continue his egotistical life-style even while married. The court ledgers are replete with cases of this kind. The attitude

of the son of the Sultan, husband of Aisha, depicts the response of
all too many real-life husbands to their marital state.

Similarly, paternity brings additional responsibilities with it, but
like marriage, it need not be instrumental to a young man's
settling down. A man might align himself with his children at the
time of their births because he believes them to be his children.
He might also tie himself to his wife, even if she is wayward,
because she is the one who has borne him those daughters and
sons. Such ties remain always contingent, however, because they
are a product of the mind, as Moroccans say, and not of the heart.
To the degree that paternity remains unprovable, paternal and
conjugal allegiances are also uncertain.

In effect, a man's pathway to responsibility and wisdom has no
certain starting points. Duties and cares weigh him down increasingly from the moment of marriage, but again duties need never
be assumed. Indeed, according to belief, responsibility is lacking
among most adult men to sufficient degree, much as it is among
most adult women. As one elderly man put it: "Few are the men,
old or young, who have accepted responsibility." Then he moved
on to his own situation as a case in point: "I, too, am among them.
You see that woman over there; I must continually have her." His
male audience nodded in sympathetic agreement.

Given the uncertain origins of male responsibility, it is not
surprising that most men are said to reach their quota of 'aqel
(intelligence, responsibility) relatively late in life. Its flowering is
believed to begin at the earliest at age forty, when a context that is
maximally conducive to the development of responsibility tends
to take place. At that age, the man has married and has generally
sired children. More importantly, his father has often given over
the extended family's control, when the household is of that form.
In effect, he is caught up in social circumstances which present
alternatives among which he sometimes chooses favorably: he
can wallow in his egotism, turning away from responsibility and

seeking satisfaction where he can most easily find it, or he can ponder the meaning of his new status, can accept his responsibilities, and can seek to overcome his own ultimate helplessness with the aid of a force external to him, the power of Allah.

Because men are thrust into a context which is maximally conducive to moral development at about forty years, many Moroccans believe that they can judge the direction of a man's later life from his behavior at that age. If a man is wise and responsible during his forties, for example, it is believed that he will likely continue in that wisdom, perhaps even adding to it little by little. By contrast, if he rejects the path of wisdom at forty or fifty, he is felt unlikely ever to achieve it; he will become the *shibani* (old man) whom people ridicule because of his lack of control over body, family, and soul: the man who visits prostitutes even though his hair is graying, the husband who deserts his wife or continually divorces without cause.

What kinds of responses are characteristic of the wise and responsive man at age forty and onward? What kind of life does a man lead once wisdom has been attained? The wise man finds, first and foremost, that body must wait upon soul. Animal responses must be tempered in the interests of social responsiveness. The goal is not to deny his bodily desires but rather to compartmentalize these and other feelings. Since it is ultimately a product of the will rather than of instinct, however, this compartmentalization is difficult, few men ever exhibiting the moral strength to attain it. Representative of this more selective category of men is the killer of ninety-nine souls, a compulsive murderer who turns to Allah late in an otherwise unsavory life. His conversion occurs when he sees the goodness of another saintly personage and when circumstances thrust upon him the obligations of host. The acceptance of the social role precedes the rejection of his murderous tendencies and the abeyance of his conjugal relationship in favor of more lofty goals. Informants declare that the murderer likely returned to his wife once Allah's wishes were made known to him, but that he likely continued to live a life of religiosity. He thereby achieved the compartmentalization ideal for his age.

Tale 22: The Murderer of Ninety-nine Souls

A man killed ninety-nine souls and needed another to finish one hundred. One day, a stranger knocked at his door and asked to stay for the night. Said the wife of the murderer: "You cannot stay, for my husband has killed ninety-nine and is searching for the hundredth." Said the stranger, who was a saint: "Guest of God (a phrase which carries a curse if the wish is not obeyed), let me stay, for there is nothing but wilderness outside. I will not be a bother. I will climb down your well and stay there for the night." Said the woman: "If God is with you, you will survive. If not, let it be known that I warned you."

That night, the murderer returned home. "Someone has been here," he immediately said. His wife answered "No one." Again he asked, this time threatening to kill his wife if she did not reply truthfully: "Who has been here?" To this she responded that someone had come and had asked to stay overnight, invoking the name of God. Fearing her husband's wrath, she had agreed to hide the man in the well.

"Climb out of the well," the murderer called to the stranger. The latter responded "in the name of God" and climbed out. Then the murderer said: "Never has anyone come to me saying 'in the name of God.' Stay and be welcome."

The saint stayed three days. Then, when he was about to leave, the murderer asked him: "I have killed ninety-nine souls. How can I find God?" Said the saint: "Go out and look for Him, and you will find Him." With that, the saint took the bones of the ram that had been sacrificed for his dinners, put them into its skin, and kicked it. The ram reappeared. Seeing this miracle, the murderer began his search for God, imbued with a new faith.

On the road, he met a man lying in the sand. The man in the sand asked the murderer where he was going. "I am going to find Allah and to ask Him where my home is in hell." Said the man in the sand, "I used to steal. Now I have nothing, and so I lie in the sand. If you find God, also ask Him where my home is in hell."

The murderer agreed and went on his way. Soon he found a man wrapped in a mat. The man in the mat asked where the traveler was headed. "I am going to find Allah and to ask Him where my place in hell is." "What did you do?" asked the man in the mat. "I killed ninety-nine souls," said the murderer. Volunteered the man in the mat, "I killed sixty souls and I stole until I had nothing, and so now I hide in a mat that I stole from a mosque. If you find Allah, ask Him where my home in hell is."

The traveler agreed and went on his way. Finally, he came to a man praying. And that man asked, "Where are you going?" "I am looking for God in order to find my home in hell." Said the man, "Stay and rest for the night."

And that man had prayed for the forty years of his life, each day beneath a tree in the distance. And each of those days, a barley bread was lowered to him along with a bunch of black grapes. That night, however, God lowered one barley bread and one wheat bread, and a bunch of black grapes and a bunch of white ones. The worshipper took the wheat bread and the white grapes and gave the barley bread and the black grapes to his guest.

After three days of resting, the traveler prepared to go on his way. His host said good-bye, and added: "If you find God, ask Him where my home in heaven is."

The murderer agreed and left. Finally, he came to Saint Gabriel on the road. Gabriel asked the traveler where he was going, and the traveler answered, "I am looking for God in order to find out where my home in hell is. Also I found a brother in the sand, and one in a mat, and they also want to know for themselves. Finally, I found a worshiper, and he wanted to know about his place in heaven." Gabriel said that he would ask God and would return the next day.

The next day, Gabriel brought the answer. The man in the sand was commanded to get out of the sand: he would be clothed and forgiven. The thief in the mat was commanded to return the mat to the mosque, and he also would be forgiven and clothed. The servant of God, however, would find no place in heaven. Instead he would take the house in hell that the murderer had previously earned, for he had taken his guest's bread and grapes.

The murderer of ninety-nine souls returned along his route, and brought the news to all who had asked him. The two thieves were joyous; the worshiper cried and cried, but God's word would not be changed.

The murderer's quest for Allah, like other affirmations of male religiosity, brings the chain of lessening male dependence upon women to a close. In early childhood a boy is totally dependent upon mother, grandmother, or sister. In adolescence, he partially asserts his independence from family, but then immediately falls into dependence upon other women, the objects of his sexual desires. His sexuality leaves him shackled whether within or outside the bounds of marriage. Indeed, it is only when women's influence is willfully restricted through a heightened realization of God's prior importance that men can reach the rarely achievable state of self-awareness that the murderer attains.

To identify the meaning of true self-awareness and self-realization in the Moroccan mode, then, one does best to consider the truly religious man: the saint, the true saintly follower, or the true pilgrim or *ḥajj* (*l-ḥajj* be *l-maʿaqul*), When one examines the lives of these men, one finds that they are at once indisputably mortal and supernaturally involved. Unlike the Christian saint, who shows his religiosity by perfecting an otherworldly life-style, or the Muslim female saint, who best maintains her saintliness if her sexuality is suppressed, the Muslim male saint or devout continues to indulge in earthly pleasures while also serving his God. Muhammad, the Prophet, took and kept a total of thirteen wives through the years of his holiness: yet Roudaniyin perceive no conflict of interest in his life. The saint Si Hmed Tijaniy held onto his riches as he pursued the pathway to grace: his followers, members of the Tijaniy brotherhood, continue to regard their own personal wealth as supportive rather than inimical to religious responsibility. Moulay Abdulqadar, founder of the Jilaliy brotherhood and predominant saint of the poor in the south of Morocco, displayed his personal wealth (according to the following tale) and otherwise demonstrated his power and success in the human world. More importantly, however, he, like these other men, was always able to put aside his earthly pleasures when the occasion merited it, taking on poverty as circumstances demanded in the service of Allah and humankind.

Tale 23: Moulay Abdulqadar

Moulay Abdulqadar was well known as a saint, with many people remembering him by visiting his tomb. So also did one woman. Her husband wanted a son, but she always bore girls. Finally, he vowed that if she bore him another girl, he would repudiate her. Fearful, she went to the tomb of Moulay Abdulqadar to pray. She prayed, "Moulay Abdulqadar, give me a son; Moulay Abdulqadar, give me a son" (whereas she should have said "Moulay Abdulqadar, intercede with Allah to give me a son"). Each day she implored him. Since a boy was already in her womb, however, the saint did not need to respond to her prayers.

Finally, after months of praying, a girl child was born. Allah had changed the boy into a girl because the woman had prayed wrongly. Shortly thereafter the man divorced his wife.

Moulay Abdulqadar saw this and showed anger. But Allah responded, *l-qaḍar ʿala ʿabdelqaḍar* (the Powerful over the servant of the Powerful). The saint, however, would not be assuaged. Again Allah said, "The Powerful over the servant of the Powerful," but the saint would not be assuaged. Moulay Abdulqadar stayed angry. For days he prayed each of his prayers on one foot, and wore rags although he was wealthy through his *baraka* (power). Finally, Allah came to him and conceded, saying that the saint could have anything that he wanted, for his abnegation caused Allah pain. With that, the saint stopped praying on one foot, wore fine clothes again, and made peace.

It is likewise with the true saintly follower or true *ḥajj*. Although each should pursue Allah zealously, he need not deny his bodily desires and needs. Rather these cravings should be relocated in time and space so as not to interfere with the priority of worship. This reorientation is particularly important with regard to sexual needs. A devotee should not shift his eyes toward women during his religious observances, for example, whether at home, in the mosque, or in the brotherhood houses, for such behavior reduces the ritual's efficacy. One saintly personage, an elder of his community, elaborated further on this notion in terms of how he ordered his personal life: a holy life necessitates sexual moderation, he said; to this end, a truly religious man should have sexual intercourse only once in a half-month.

What is revealed in the lives of the Prophet, the saints, and their most perfect followers, then, is not a changeless outline for religious behavior but rather a flexibility of attitude, one that combines a lack of compulsiveness about bodily urges with an ongoing responsiveness to the religious needs of community and self. Holiness becomes a product of the mind and of the will, with mind and will sensitively determining what is laudable and necessary in a worldly interpersonal life.

Thus the murderer of ninety-nine souls takes the first step toward holiness when he rejects his homicidal compulsion and forfeits his need for conjugality in order to search for Allah, but he has not yet achieved an ever-flexible but stressless balance in organizing his life. By contrast, we know that holiness in no way resides in the self-righteous adherent of forty years, for he cannot put off his cravings even when faced with an important religious task: the sustenance and support of a new convert. The receipt of the forty-year-long gift, the grapes and bread, does not give proof of his holiness; rather his holiness is disproved through his discomfort with giving the best when the murderer is in need.

The conscious taking on and putting off of earthly pleasures, which true religious life implies, gives an insight into the dynamics of Ramadan, the Muslim month of fast. A Muslim must forego food, drink, and sex during the daylight hours of each day of the Ramadan month from approximately the years of puberty onward. The comprehensive fast ends with each sunset, so that satiation is allowable but only at preordained times. The fast thereby teaches that bodily desires must be resituated (although not negated) in the light of external religious requirements. Additionally, it shows that cravings generally outweigh actual need and capacity, for the Moroccan buys much food during the daylight hours but can eat only little upon breaking the fast. Similarly, sexual desires pass less noticed as generalized fasting becomes an all-consuming concern. The fast, one might conjecture, serves as one training ground for learning to subordinate bodily desires and for realizing that all desires are mutable. In essence, it emerges as a training ground for life in the male saintly mode.

I say male saintly mode because women who fast cannot take on and put off the fasting requirements totally through will, as men can. However strong woman's religiosity, her menstruation or her past menstrual history necessarily renders her months of religious devotion less elegantly performed. Women do not fast on the days of their periods; even were they to fast out of personal ardor, those days do not enter into the holy tabulation. Instead women must make up their menstruation days by fasting equivalently in other months. Interestingly, many women are believed to be underhanded even in how these days are chosen: the clever and egotistical woman is said to select short winter days to complete her fasting obligation.

Men are not restricted by such physiological encumbrances. Rather, for them life in a religious mode arises from the spiritual self. This makes it all the more precious: neither inevitable in its occurrence nor easily accomplished, it gains through the effort that it requires.

Chapter Six

MOTHER AND FATHER
IN COUNTERPOINT

PARENTHOOD AND THE
SEPARATION OF THE SEXES

There is a telling omission in the code of personal statute that was framed for the Moroccan nation just after independence. Article 99 lists those persons who are to be called upon as caretakers for children in the event that the children's parents are divorced. The sequence is a detailed one that was set out by certain legal scholars in Islam's first centuries. For those cases in which caretakers must be found, ibn Malik, forefather of the Malikite rite, Morocco's legal tradition, laid out these priorities (Bousquet 1958: 13): first the mother, then the mother's ancestresses, then the mother's sister, then the father's ancestresses, then the father, the sister, the father's sister, or others would be appointed. The 1957–58 code reproduces this sequence almost exactly except for the omission of one major category: the father is left out.

What is the meaning of this "inadvertence of the legislator" (Colomer 1963: 178)? Apart from showing that the code was elaborated somewhat precipitously, it seems to indicate that Moroccans associate fathers with child care only minimally. Fathers are the recognized authority figures within any Moroccan family; they are the social system's first choice as legal guardians (*wali,* pl. *awliya*). Child care, however, is viewed as being chiefly a female preoccupation, and men, as such, should not normally take part in these tasks.

In effect, two realms of involvement with children are set out in the law code, one associated predominantly with men, the other predominantly with women. Fathers are first expected to support their children financially. Fathers (or the persons that fathers or the courts appoint in fathers' absence) also take on the role of legal guardian; this means that they administer property on children's behalf. Third, they take on the responsibility of matrimonial spokesman: they can represent their sons and must represent their virginal daughters at the negotiation of marriage contracts. In short, the father's arena centers upon the economic aspects of life and then radiates out from it. The mother's arena, by contrast, centers upon caretaking: protecting the child, nurturing it, and assuring that it will grow in accordance with its best interests and needs.

The law code sets out a division of parental labor, but it also affirms that both men and women might be capable of assuming the responsibilities generally associated with the opposite sex. Fathers (or certain other men) can be named to the caretaker role: article 99 proves this. Similarly, mothers (or other properly qualified females) can be named as legal guardians for children, and in the case of her husband's indigence, a mother is expected to provide for her children's sustenance if she is economically secure or productive. Indeed, of the legally specified roles that men assume, only that of matrimonial guardian is forbidden to women.

This is expectable because it is the one role that would throw women into unavoidably direct and public exchanges with males.

This ultimate flexibility in parental division of labor partially explains why some women are lauded for going out into the world beyond the household and performing "male" tasks. Women can properly take full-time jobs and go to court if they have no sons, fathers, or husbands who can act on their behalf. If their demeanor is modest—if they rush to work and back, all the while avoiding the looks of men, for example—their intrusion into the male sphere is deemed appropriate and acceptable. The same behavior tends to be differently evaluated, however, if the adventurous woman shuns the support of capable males. In cases in which women work for their own pocket money or for their own pleasure, many onlookers characterize their work as improper, dangerous, inappropriate, or frivolous.

The occurrence of these flexibilities and rigidities in and about behavior underscores an essential organizational point: a strict parental division of labor in the Moroccan family most often occurs when husband-wife (or male-female) pairs are intact, and, indeed, seems to be tied to attitudes about male-female sociality more than to attitudes about child rearing. Children tend to be allocated to women's sphere, and so men are bound to interact with children only in certain ways, for they and women must generally situate themselves apart. If either the male or female presence is removed, however, the possibility of greater behavioral flexibility emerges: women can take on the roles of provider and administrator and men can become the caretakers of children.

Separation of the sexes thus promotes a distancing of fathers from children, at least during their children's early years. Informants' statements imply this. I asked my neighbor Omar when it was that he spent time with the children that he always said that he loved. "At mealtimes," was his first answer. (Meals are shared by husband, wife, and children if the family is nuclear. Otherwise men eat apart from women and small children. This separation also occurs when there are guests.) Why did he not remain home with them after dinner; why did he return to his shop to spend more time with his friends? "Why should I stay home with women? What can I say to them?" was his answer. The limited time accorded to his children was associated with the father's desire to stay apart from the women of his house.

The pressure that many men feel for preserving their masculine identities by fraternizing with men and by remaining outside the home, then, indicates a male-female tension rather than a fundamental estrangement from children. This fact is crucial to a proper appreciation of the emotional relationship of father to child. Fathers can be seen carrying their small sons and daughters and often play with their small children at mealtimes. In these instances, paternal affection tends to be marked, even though total time spent with those children is small. Moreover, fathers sometimes willingly take on parental tasks that are generally associated with women if women are busy or absent, a pattern for which the following early parental experience of Ali and his wife, Rqiya, provides one case in point. It concerns sleeping patterns. Moroccan children generally sleep next to their mothers, while fathers sleep apart. Thus a first child sleeps by its mother's side, nursing at will from her breast. A second child replaces the first child next to the mother, the elder one being relegated to a once-removed position. This sleep sequence is rather predictable, with children fanning out concentrically from the mother according to age. When Rqiya gave birth to her second child, she appropriately arranged her two children in this fashion. Her first child, however, reacted badly to the distancing: the baby cried and would not be quieted. So Ali offered to sleep with the older child while Rqiya remained with the newborn infant. The one pair slept on one side of the room while the second pair slept on the other. Ali, Rqiya, and the now adult firstborn still recall his decision with satisfaction and pride.

The attachment that fathers feel for their children is sometimes so strong that it holds marriages together. A man is less likely to repudiate his wife once children are born: he might even endure a conjugal life that is fraught with difficulty in order to preserve parental ties. Both men and women acknowledge that men can be strongly influenced by these considerations. Since men can divorce easily, since no alimony exists, and since child support payments tend to be minimal, economic advantage seems not to be primary in holding these relationships together. Instead the glue appears to be fatherly sentiments.

TIME, SPACE, AND MOTHER'S POWER

However warmly fathers regard their children, it is nonetheless the case that small children situate themselves in the kitchen or the courtyard with their mothers and other women, and so intensive father-child interactions perforce remain few. Mothers and other females tend to care for small children almost exclusively and so come to have an overriding influence over them. For their part, fathers feel affection for their offspring but tend to stay emotionally tangential because they remain apart.

This arrangement gives mothers de facto control over children and makes them wielders of considerable powers which at first glance might seem more appropriate to men. Often mothers are the ultimate decision-makers about children's futures and welfare, rather than fathers, children's de jure guardians. Mothers are sometimes the guiding forces in promoting their children's education. They are also their children's primary protectors, defending their children against outside aggressors, even though fathers, who range more freely outside the household, might more appropriately serve in that capacity. Thus mothers often fight bitterly with the mothers of children who attack their offspring. Fathers, who tend to hear about these injustices some hours later, typically regard these street altercations as inappropriate, embarrassing, and uncontrolled. They take them as proof of the passionate but disruptive tendencies of women.

The fact that parental powers tend to concentrate in the hands of women has its sterner side, for mothers are also their children's chief disciplinarians. Fathers occasionally punish, sometimes with considerable pomp, but mothers dole out daily rewards and punishments. They pinch, throw things, or slap, but more often threaten or cajole. "Just wait," is a common threat forwarded by women who are otherwise occupied with work or who are seated too comfortably to go after a culprit. The phrase also reveals a certain very real impotence, particularly when it is leveled at sons, for boys can simply run out of the house and thereby escape mothers' control.

Many mothers call upon beings and forces outside themselves as they threaten children with disciplinary action for their misdeeds. There is the beetle; there is the donkey of the cemetery; there is Aisha Qandisha, who is half woman, half monster; all are ready to attack. There is also the hapless guest, and sometimes the anthropologist, who suddenly is portrayed as wrathfully just. He or she carries a beetle and is ready to loose it; he or she might carry a pair of scissors or a knife and is ready to use them to punish wayward boys who have experienced the trauma of circumcision some weeks or months back.

The use of indirection in these instances indicates that mothers wish not to jeopardize the other part of their identity: their images as loving, caring, and protective beings. It also indicates that mothers fear that children's love and loyalty can be lost. Mothers fight for their children; they tend to use innumerable strategies in order to protect them. They truly make sacrifices. "The child that loses its mother has nothing," says one Moroccan proverb; in it, the messages of maternal involvement and filial appreciation are marked. And yet children's professions of love often do not provide sufficient solace to the mother. In a society in which women are separated from their loving kin upon marriage, in which husbands tend to be distant and often unsympathetic, and in which children become women's primary source of love, women tend to seize upon filial love as their mainstay and harbor fears concerning the loss of it.

This freneticism spells difficulty for mothers and children alike. Mothers are dependent upon their children for love and for support in old age, and so try strongly to maintain children's allegiance. But in attempting to do so, mothers are also likely to become possessive. The stereotypic mother-in-law, or 'aguz, for example, is said to be difficult because she sees her son's wife as a competitor and so strikes out against her, seeking to contain her influence by denigrating her, for the mother fears loss. The stereotype pertains to only one facet of the mother-in-law–daughter-in-law relationship, but the syndrome occurs often and provides insights into the dangers that mothers feel that they face. Correspondingly, a son typically finds himself pulled in two directions— toward his bride and toward his mother—after entering into marriage. Often married in order to pacify his parents and paired with a woman who is his mother's choice, the son later discovers that his marriage nonetheless does not totally please his mother. Instead, no matter how hard he tries to be a loving son, he causes her pain.

Children thus react to their mothers with a complex array of responses and sentiments. They see their mothers as their primary source of emotional and nurturant support, and yet they also resent and resist these women as disciplinarians. Fear mingles with love. From another perspective, children's love is strong, but children also fear the loved one's loss. Here, love comes to be coupled with anxiety. Too, there is the comfort of being loved well but also the burden of being loved too compulsively. This weighs upon both daughters and sons, but particularly haunts sons' adult days.

One exchange that the woman Habiba had with her five-year-old daughter Aisha illustrates the ambivalence that surfaces on both sides. Aisha had been willful, and Habiba sought to punish. She began, however, by teasing, pinching very slightly, while commenting on Aisha's stubborn streak. Aisha first responded with laughter. Then the punishment continued and the pinches crossed the boundary from pleasure to pain. Aisha's face froze, and she was silent: she cried a moment after, but at first did not know whether to laugh or cry from the attention. The mother projected love and anger; the daughter responded first with love that later intermingled with the fear of betrayal.

MATERNAL IMAGES

The comprehensiveness of the mother's functions and the complexity of feelings associated with it bring considerable strain to bear upon the mother-child relationship. Not unexpectedly, this strain, with its undercurrent of negativism, is revealed in various kinds of discourse. Indeed, the negative component becomes a folkloric emphasis. Mothers exhibit their frailty in the tales; they endanger their children by perpetuating ignorance and by yielding to temptation. Initially caring, they turn away from even their caretaking chores. Only 7 of the 31 maternal characterizations in the 95 tales collected by this anthropologist involve positive deeds by mothers, while 2 are neutral and 22 are negative.

The 22 negative delineations depict betrayal in process, betrayal which is petty in origin and brutal in its result. Mothers do not reject their children in response to inescapable dilemmas in which child neglect becomes one of several unhappy life options. Instead, maternal disloyalty is triggered by less laudable drives. In the tales, food, wealth, and sexual satisfaction are the benefits which the mother most often seeks when she turns her back on her child.

The mother, says the folklore, searches for these benefits for herself alone. Then, when she has obtained them, she finds them insufficient. In the tale of the lamb hocks (tale 8), the mother desires a taste of her son-in-law's supper, although both daughter and mother are provided each evening with a full kilo of meat. The man eventually divorces the daughter because of the mother's bad influence. In the tale of the boy and the girl (tale 13), the mother, like the father who acquiesces to her, compulsively desires the children's extra pigeon. The children are subjected to their encounter with the witch because of the lure of the extra meat. In the following tale, the mother gains silver through a chance discovery but remains dissatisfied with her windfall. Her desire for more silver results in the bizarre and symbolic death of her son.

Tale 24: The Mother at Ergita

At Ergita in the mountains, there is a saintly tomb of the kind to which people went in the olden days in order to hide their money. One day in more recent years, a slave girl was gathering wood and entered the Ergita tomb to rest. She was carrying her baby son on her back. There in the tomb she came upon a cache of money. She took some of the silver, but then wanted more of it. So she put down her son and substituted silver, filling up the cloth on her back. With that, she hurried off, leaving her son on the ground. When she returned, she found that the tomb's walls had closed together mysteriously. Her son had been squeezed to the top of the rampart where the form of the child's body still can be seen, immortalized in stone.

Food and money are strongly desired by mothers, but the strongest of a mother's desires, imply the tales, remains sexuality. The following tale underscores the strength of a mother's sexual motivation. The wife of a *hajj,* or pilgrim, succumbs to the advances of a *hartani,* a brown man of servile status. The *hartani* lacks whiteness, the essential mark of beauty; he is servile hereditarily, and so cannot achieve social success. And yet the wife of the well-to-do pilgrim forfeits all her social advantages, leaves her children, and flouts social convention. She matches the *hartani,* whose essence is believed to be animalistic: her blood, like his, proves to be "hot."

Tale 25: The Pilgrim's Wife and the Ḥartani

Two friends went on the pilgrimage to Mecca, leaving their wives behind for the many months during which they traveled by camel. Each wife was to stay secluded until her husband's return. One wife, however, went out almost immediately, disobeying her husband's wishes. The second wife, remained at home until l-'id ṣ-ṣghir, the second most important religious holiday for Muslims. Then that woman, named Ayyasha, dressed up and went out to the streets, where she came upon a *hartani* whom she desired.

Several months later, the two pilgrims returned. The first cursed his wife's disloyalty and quickly married another woman. Ayyasha's husband, however, became sad when he found that his wife was gone. He feared that she might be sick, dead, or dying. So he cried and cried, and then began to care for the children that his wife had left behind.

One night while he was sleeping, the pilgrim heard a knock at his door. He asked who it was. "Sidi u Sidi" (the patron saint of Taroudannt), a voice answered. The pilgrim did not open the door but listened to the message: "Ayyasha is in the house of a *hartani* named *flan*" (literally, so-and-so). The pilgrim then fell back to sleep. The next day he prayed and proceeded with life as usual.

A second night, the pilgrim slept, and the saint approached him while sleeping. Again he said, "Ayyasha is in the house of a *hartani* named *flan.*" The next morning the pilgrim cried for Ayyasha, prayed, and continued to proceed with life as usual.

Finally the saint visited a third time and delivered his message. This time the pilgrim went to his wife's two brothers and repeated the dream. Then, the three men climbed onto the roof next to the ḥarṭani's house. There, from the rooftop they could see Ayyasha working.

The two brothers shot Ayyasha dead. As for the ḥarṭani, he was taken to prison. The pilgrim, for his part, took another wife.

This tale implies much about the place Moroccans give sexuality in the maternal psyche. Moroccans cite maternity as women's ultimate calling, and yet the importance of maternity to women is ever unsure. The mother shows love and concern for her children when temptations are lacking: this is recognized. It is feared, however, that maternal feelings will be shoved into the background as temptations appear. In effect, sexuality and maternity are depicted as vying, with the one registering gains as the other suffers loss.

This limited good notion of lovingness is nicely reflected in Moroccans' beliefs about the sorcery of women. The woman who desires a man's sexual favors can use many kinds of sorcery in order to ensnare him. She can fashion wicks out of the cloth with which he wipes his genitals after intercourse and then can burn them in a jar with honey, clarified butter, and male spices (those which are phallus-shaped). A wick is burned in this way each day for seven days. (This practice calls to mind the traditional women's sorcery of the marriage week. At that time, women burn seven wicks over the seven-day marriage period so that the groom will be solicitous.) The seven wicks and the other ingredients can also be put into a can, which is then placed in a charcoal burner and covered with ash; the can is left to smolder as food burns above it. Or, most potent of all, the woman might wear a piece of cloth that has been dipped in the blood of someone who died accidentally and tragically: this cloth is generally worn around the neck inside a ṣerra, or pouch.

Each of these mechanisms is used to win over men and to hold them. Each is believed to be powerful and efficacious. Each, however, is believed to cause grave illness or death to infants if they are near. The infant is said to lose weight: his cranium separates, his head swells, and his brain drops when he smells these aphrodisiacs. Indeed, the smelling of the fumes *(shemman)* is cited as the cause of death for most infants aged under two years.

Once maternity and sexuality are seen as contending forces, women's and children's well-being come to stand forever at odds. Indeed it is only during pregnancy, when mother and child are physically one, that this conflict of interests is obviated. Significantly, men sometimes forget the temporary respite from a putatively overpowering sexuality that pregnancy is believed to afford: they are often, too, caught up in the image of women's sexuality and egotism. Such an oversight occurs in the tale of the butcher that follows. Note that the pregnant wife's craving for food comes to be magnified into a desire for sexuality and so is immediately suspect. Tragedy is the result.

Tale 26: The Butcher

There once was a woman who was pregnant by her difficult husband. One day, as she was walking home past a butcher shop, she craved a piece of meat. Looking at a piece of liver, she murmured to herself that she desired it. The butcher heard these words and fulfilled her wishes (for it is good to give a pregnant woman what she desires, since it is said to be her stomach that desires it). Indeed, he gave her all the internal organs of a newly slaughtered sheep.

Some of the husband's friends, however, were watching and brought him the news. When the husband heard the news, he supposed that the butcher was enamored of his wife. To punish her, he bought a sheep, slaughtered it, and insisted that his wife should eat all of it in one sitting, even if it caused her demise.

The wife ate and ate, until she could eat no further. Then she pleaded, saying that she could eat no more. But the husband would not be dissuaded. Angered, he took a dagger and slit open her stomach. There, in her innards, he found his child with a piece of the butcher's liver still in its teeth.

When the washers of the dead came for the dead woman's body, they found that it was gone. In the woman's place, they found a pair of silver scissors, the ones that the angels had used to cut her garments for the afterlife. They had left them behind as a sign that she had been taken directly to heaven, for she had done no earthly wrong.

The ultimate measure of maternal betrayal, however, lies in the distress and dislocation that it causes. The Taroudannt folklore implies that these negative effects are marked and recurring: several mothers cause or seek the deaths of their children (tales 13, 24); one causes her children's incarceration underground (tale 3); yet another prevents her son's resurrection (tale 9); still another causes her child's discomfort in the afterlife (tale 28), while the mother who prays to Moulay Abdulqadar (tale 23) causes a change in the child's sex (to female, which must be taken as negative). Given this emphasis, not only does the possibility of maternal rejection haunt the Moroccan child; it also suggests the trauma of severe survival threats.

Almost as detrimental is the impact that the folkloric mother has upon her child's social world. Several mothers precipitate their daughters' divorces (e.g., tale 8), while another causes her daughter's temporary fall from wifely grace (tale 35); in many, a son experiences intense shame when his mother's sexual passion is revealed to him and outsiders (e.g., tales 17, 27). The following tale illustrates the depth of resentment that such a revelation causes.

Tale 27: Sidi bu Ḥṣira (Saint of the Mat)

There once was a man whose mother, sister, and wife all lived with him. When the mother prayed, she asked for a husband. When the sister prayed, she asked for the family's shepherd as a spouse. When the wife prayed, she asked that her husband might be blinded so that her lover might freely enter the house. One day, an old woman—a *mwa 'aguz*—brought the news of their praying. The man, however, was skeptical and asked to hear for himself. So the old woman counseled: "Tell your women that a saint exists in the forest who satisfies everyone's wishes. His name is Sidi bu Hsira (the saint of the mat), for he dwells in a mat which must never be touched. They will want to go to him immediately. Then take a mat to the forest and wrap yourself in it. From the mat, you will hear them reveal their deepest desires."

The man told the women about the saint, and immediately they asked to visit him. The mother said that she wished to pray for her health. The sister said that she wished to ask for her brother's protection. The wife said that she would pray for her husband's long life. The man acquiesced in their demands and raced off to the wilderness with his mat.

First, the mother approached the "holy" place. She said: "Allah care for us and give me a man to help me share the silver that I have hidden for my old age." Then the sister approached and asked for her brother's good health and for the shepherd in marriage. Finally, the wife gave her request: "Strike down my husband with blindness so that I can bring in my lover." With that, the three women returned to the house.

The next day the man searched out the shepherd and arranged his sister's marriage. Then he called to his mother and told her that she too would be wed. The woman gasped, protested, but then agreed, saying that a husband would aid her in her prayers.

The following afternoon, the man told his mother to go to the bath to wash for her wedding night. "Today I shiver; tomorrow I dress finely," she said as she poured the cold water over her body. Then she perfumed herself in preparation for her new spouse.

That night, the man took his mother to a lion's den, saying that she would be meeting her new husband there. "He comes with candles," noted the mother as she spotted the lion's eyes. "This is true love," said she as it began to nibble on her neck. Soon afterward, she was dead.

As to the sister, she married the shepherd. The wife, for her part, was forced out of the house and sent a letter of divorce.

The tale of Sidi bu Hsira is interesting because of its comparative message. Three stages of female sexuality confront the man in the tale, and he responds differentially according to the psychic pain that each affords. He satisfies his sister's innocent longing, for there is no treachery in it: she naïvely supposes that her loyalty to family and her desire for a mate can co-occur. Somewhat magnanimously, he repudiates his wife as punishment for her powerful and illicit adult sexual urge. As son, however, he is unmitigatingly harsh: he condemns his mother's desire for married sex (along with her petty pilfering) more severely than the treachery of his wife.

The severity of the man's reaction in the tale of Sidi bu Hṣira reflects deep fears of maternal betrayal. Folklorically, the concern is a recurrent one. The tale is unrepresentative of the larger folk corpus, however, in the sense that the son exacts his punishment in addition to pondering it. More often, the child suffers while the mother remains unrestrained and untouched. In fact, rarely does a folkloric child take definitive action against its mother: in Sidi bu Hṣira, the mother is killed, although significantly not by the son's hand; in the tale of Eve's children (tale 3), she and womankind are punished, this time by Allah, who makes parturition difficult.

Let us return to the second case, for the Moroccan image of the mother can best be understood through a reconsideration of the first mother, Eve. Eve, it will be remembered, loved her children but desired them unequally. She cherished the prettiest. That attraction, however, led her not to nurture her children but ultimately to destroy them. Through her covetousness, Eve hid away her most beloved children, thereby causing them to be fitful and physically frail. Finally, when she admitted to their existence, she did so for her own welfare, not theirs.

The Eve tale provides its clue to the contradictions inherent in the mother as folk character. Maternal love seeks to imprison; it attempts to return the child to the mother's all-encompassing control. Its thrust is to the womb. As such, it is ultimately the most antisocial of motivations. And yet maternity is also socially necessary. It increases the populace; it forms a precondition for new social relations. Maternity both creates and endangers the world's social equilibrium. No wonder that its occurrence is viewed as at once wonderful and threatening.

PATERNAL IMAGES

If the Taroudannt folklore reveals deep-seated fears regarding the loss of the mother, it also reveals concurrent hopes for compensatory love from a second source. If the mother is lost or if she chooses to withhold herself, the child best serves himself by having an emotionally satisfying recourse. The father, intermittently affectionate during the child's early years, provides one viable substitute.

The father emerges as an essentially positive figure in folkloric discourse. He is thoughtful, positively concerned, and responsible. Often, he is a constant provider; typically, he exhibits moderation that culminates in efficacious behavior; frequently, he is a careful advisor to his daughters and sons. His protective urge reaches out even to those daughters whom marriage has taken from him. As could be expected, this behavior conforms to the more general male moral dynamic. Initially cool toward his offspring, the father comes to admit his failings vis-à-vis his children and thereafter displays heightened concern.

In the end, a mother, even when positively motivated, cannot compare to her husband, her children's father, in the parental realm. In the following tale, the mother's apparently positive instincts nonetheless place substantial obstacles in the heavenly pathway of her dead child. The child's suffering is finally ameliorated through the father's rationality and wisdom.

Tale 28: The Tears

There was a man who was learned and religious. He told his wife: "When you give birth, do not cry if the baby dies." One day, the wife gave birth to a son. It died and she did not cry. A while later, she gave birth, again to a son. It also died, and she did not cry. A third time she gave birth. And when that baby died, the sadness stayed with her. She cried three tears, then quickly wiped her face dry.

When her husband entered the room, he asked her if she had cried, and she answered that she hadn't. Then he told her to close her eyes (for he knew well that she had shed tears). Closing her eyes, she found herself in the afterlife. There the Angel of Death called to her first son: *"wa flan bin flana"* (O, John Doe, son of Jane Doe), and the son came quickly—clean, fat, and dressed nicely. Then he called to the second son: *"wa flan bin flana,"* and he also came quickly—clean, healthy, and well-dressed. But when he called to the third son, no one answered or came to him. The angel called again and then again. Finally a child—worn, ill-clad, and dirty—arrived. "Why are you not like your brothers?" the mother scolded. The youngest son answered: "The three tears that you cried became three rivers to cross." With that, the mother opened her eyes upon the real world. And from that day, when her children died, she never wept again.

However strong be the child's wish for the father, the realities of life also push a child to react ambivalently toward him. Childhood brings a taste of the intimate father, but it also creates a stronger, more ongoing image of the father as stern, distant parent. There is physical distance: the father typically remains absent from the household through major portions of each day in his child's life. A young child endures it, while an older child can at best bridge the geographical gap by going out to him. This, of course, is an impossibility for a daughter for reasons of modesty, and can, in fact, be only partially implemented by sons. Even into adolescence, a boy is expected to serve adult males and is sometimes sent off by them to work at bothersome tasks, but he is also kept peripheral, for even adolescent boys are deemed scarcely responsible. There is also emotional distance. The father views himself as his household's supervisor and regulator and generally expects no better than childish willfulness from both women and children. He therefore feels justified in pressing his demands and chastises when obedience is not immediately forthcoming. The father might throw shoes or other objects, strike his wife and children, or shout his orders as he momentarily invades the female lifespace. His style is likely to produce a stubborn, spectacular, but ephemeral display, to which his wife and children's response is more often quiet obedience, followed frequently by mocking amusement when the father-husband is gone.

If ambivalence toward the father is engendered by the conflict of his lovingly intimate and his sternly distant images, the child's ambivalence is heightened through the complexity of the father's interactions with the child's mother, whom the child both fears and loves. In numerous ways, the father has control over the mother: he can divorce her, beat her, curtail her social relations, and withhold funds. The father sometimes uses these prerogatives to pressure the mother to remain in the home: in this her children find solace; and yet the father sometimes causes the mother unhappiness and in so doing also causes his children grief.

It can be conjectured that one aim in a male-dominated, male-oriented society is to build upon the trust-inducing image of the father so as to provide a foundation for a more general positive attitude toward men. In the Taroudannt case, this task seems less difficult, for Oedipal hostilities appear to be reduced in most families. Generally the father does not vie for the mother's affection, for most Moroccan fathers do not marry the mothers of their children out of choice or out of love. Nor does the father force a weakening of mother-child bonds: instead older siblings are forced by younger ones onto the fringes of the mother's emotional and physical lifespace. Moreover, children seldom hear their mothers refer to their fathers with love, affection, or passion.

More typically, they witness hostility, resentment, and condescension. Their fathers are called drunkards or shiftless profligates; they are sex-addicted or sexually inadequate: these are the more probable messages that mothers project as they talk about their spouses to kinswomen and friends.

As a consequence, fathers and children share a potential for becoming compatriots, a potential which fear of the mother's betrayal can drive toward actualization. They can stand together as the outside sexual world beckons to the mother and as they resolve to prevent her from acknowledging the call. The threats are sex and romance, and fears of them find strong bases in beliefs in the mother's putatively powerful sexuality. "If a woman loves a man, she will give it to him through a hole in the door" (Westermarck 1930: 82): the proverb summarizes both the child and father's fears.

Ironically, given this fear of betrayal, the phenomenon of sexual separation, which partly engenders the problem, can provide an ultimate solace for the child. Through it, the father is kept forcibly at a distance when the mother is present; but once the mother is gone, the father becomes available as loving parent. The child thus can hope for affection from one if not the other source. This hope and the fears underlying it are also reinforced by other beliefs. The mother, as woman, cannot but engage in the fall: this is culturally expectable. The father, as man, holds a potentiality for attaining wisdom, responsibility, and holiness and so can provide ultimate salvation for his child.

Appropriately, the respect for the father that results takes a form which circumvents the endangering sphere of sexuality. It evidences itself in nonsexual and antisexual behavior between fathers and sons (or daughters). Sons should not curse or smoke in the presence of their fathers. They should not talk about sex. Nor should they in any way call attention to their sexual desire. One newly married young man no longer felt comfortable eating with his father, as he had previously, for the son's sexual involvement was implicit in day-to-day affairs. Hence he would not eat when the two men were alone, and in no case would he eat with his father, mother, and wife, because of the discomfort that he felt through his wife's presence. Interestingly, he continued to eat with his mother and wife at lunchtimes without evincing shame.

What results is a kind of exchange which is different from that between mothers and sons or mothers and daughters. The father-son or father-daughter relationship finds its expression in a quasi-ethereal mode, while the mother-son or mother-daughter relationship is more earthy. When the farmer Hmed educated one male anthropologist (K. Dwyer, personal communication) about the mating process for mules, his son Sa'id bowed his head and quickly ran from the house. The boy was ashamed not before the guest but rather before his father. Later, when the father wished to talk about prostitution, he instructed his son to leave: the conversation could not proceed because of both males' embarrassment. These patterns contrast sharply with the openly sexual conversations a woman has in front of her children, whether daughters or small sons.

Concern with sexuality, of course, is implied in the very existence of stringent prohibitions of this sort. Why, then, is sexuality forced from the mind in the case of the father? Perhaps because the father initially activated the mother's sexuality. Perhaps because the father remains the mother's sexual partner. Possibly also because it is feared that the mother might eventually court familial disaster through her sexuality and the father must in no way be conceptualized as capable of going the same route.

Wishes, hopes, and fears, as they come together through the exigencies of Moroccan family life, provide an emotional base for the restructuring of children's attitudes about male and female. The mother's (female) world is passionate, but the experiencing of its particular passions provides a psychological burden. The child also looks for distance, or minimally options, and partially finds them in the father's (male) world, where there is less passion (the rather bland folkloric image of the father demonstrates this), but there is also the hope of serenity. For the boy, who must move into the male arena, and the girl, who must marry out into a world in which men hold ultimate authority, this shift in filial allegiance provides preparation for a changeover. Because of it, the child can more easily make the change from a female-dominated universe into a male-oriented world.

Chapter Seven
THE "JUSTICE"
OF SECLUSION

THREAT AND ESCAPE

In the old days, marriage was a revelation many times over. A groom saw his bride for the first time as he entered the bridal chamber after hours of feasting with friends. Wrapped in a woolen blanket and with a veil over her face, the bride sat in her corner awaiting the husband that she had never before met. Her kinswomen had led her, eyes covered, to her new home and had left her in the room that she would thereafter inhabit. In that place, never before seen by her, the groom would deflower her, turning her into a sexual being and proving her virginity to kinfolk and guests.

In those days, say old men and women who remember, brides were "glowing." They could be so, Roudaniyin are wont to say, because their life essence had been kept hidden from view. Male strangers never stole glances at them previous to marriage. Adult women, apart from immediate neighbors and relatives, rarely saw the virgins who were kept within the limits of a house, for proper girls did not go out, and when visitors came, young girls were expected to absent themselves. Even the mother of a groom, the woman who searched out a wife for him, found her daughter-in-law chiefly through hearsay, not by eye but by ear.

The need to keep a girl from "glowing" in others' eyes before her wedding affected many activities in the old days. At one time, most virgins were prohibited from going to the public baths, and indeed were sometimes told to wash thoroughly only to the elbows. In that way, they would be properly clean to do housework and yet in no way would jeopardize their beauty by allowing others to partake of it. Then when a virgin finally scrubbed herself on her wedding night, she was believed to render herself all the more precious and captivating for her spouse.

These patterns of behavior have changed now. Most virgins venture out of their houses; most grooms view their brides before the wedding night, although grooms' mothers are still apt to initiate the choice of their daughters-in-law; almost all young girls frequent the public baths. And yet a good deal of the underlying watchfulness remains for brides, grooms, and their families. The evil eye (l-'ain) threatens the good and healthy life of both sexes, with the occasional Roudaniy seeing virgins as prone to even more dangers now than before. As one Taroudannt man put it as he commented upon girls' newfound mobility: "They have become like the meat that hangs in the butcher shop. Passersby view it. How, then, can it match the meat that one can buy privately from the herder; how can it taste so sweet?"

Roudaniyin perceive "the eye" as a threat, whether they are rich or poor, whether they are educated or not in the Western style. And yet "the eye" is only one of a number of dangers with which Taroudannt dwellers feel themselves faced. Human outsiders are seen as likely to exert their wills and so force bad behavior.

And through an internal human tendency toward excess, there are also ever-present dangers from self. Nonhuman beings also threaten health, life, and happiness: there are the *jnun,* for example, Eve's underworld children, who lash out at humans because of their fitful, vengeful natures.

The quest for safety through the watchfulness of others and through personal vigilance thus becomes an important human enterprise, one that forms a major emphasis in child rearing as well as one that affects behavior choices for the adult self. The Moroccan mother carefully guards her children, first by imposing safeguards and then by teaching self-defense to her offspring. The mechanisms that mothers utilize are many, for the dangers are diverse. By extension, the adult Moroccan continues with at least a degree of this vigilance, often using the same techniques that he or she learned early in life.

One sphere in which protection is fostered even in the earliest days is in a baby's relations with self. An infant is swaddled, for example, not only to make its legs strong and straight, one common explanation for the practice, but also to prevent it from scratching its eyes out and from romping endlessly, oblivious of sleep. The child is bound with cloth from the neck down, with its arms and legs carefully folded upon one another, a practice which continues for varying time periods, depending upon the mother's inclination and the season. (Binding is terminated in the hot summer months.) Then, at various times during each day, the child is unwrapped and is briskly rubbed all over and manipulated, his mother providing him with the movement and stimulation that he otherwise lacks. In this way, isolation and contact are largely controlled by the parent, a circumstance that is deemed reasonable, for a child cannot be trusted to provide itself with care and satisfaction.

If mothers swaddle their babies in order to minimize destructive tendencies that are internally generated, they use amulets and other religious paraphernalia to ward off the onslaught of external negative powers. A ṣrira, a bundle of spices (e.g., coriander), minerals (e.g., alum, salt, sulphur), and silver, is tied around a baby's wrist or neck at birth; one might also be hung around the child's neck in later years. Each remains hanging until the threads that secure it accidentally break. The careful mother, however, does not leave her child unguarded even after a ṣrira has naturally fallen: instead she continues to replace it in order to assure continuing protection.

Saints provide benefits similar to those which a ṣrira affords. A saint is said to provide protection for his adherents by repulsing evil spirits and more occasionally by interceding with Allah (tale 23). A conscientious mother thus does well to seek out spiritual assistance of a saintly kind from the beginning. Almost all mothers do this when a child is very young. Initially, a prospective mother might send her scarf to a saint's tomb or a brotherhood house in order to obtain a handful of flour which she mixes with her soup during the perilous days after parturition. She does this in order to obtain strength for both herself and the child. Then on the fortieth day after birth, she sends her child to the saintly house and has its hair cut—in tufts, strips, pony-tails, ringlets, or these in combination—according to the saintly protector's alleged preference in style. The haircut provides an immediate signal to outsiders that a particular saint is watching, with the felt result that "the eye," evil spirits, and jnun are more effectively repulsed. And should they not be, then mothers generally revise their allegiances, aligning themselves with yet other saints, as they frantically try to protect a child that is weak, ill, or dying. In these cases, a good mother is judged not so much by her fidelity as by her responsiveness to her child's plight.

The saints provide automatic protection against evil underworld spirits and "the eye," but personal vigilance is also encouraged in children early in life. The careful Muslim child learns not to pour boiling water, transfer live coals, or enter a room, for example, without first intoning the formula "in the name of Allah" in order to ward off those spirits that might otherwise be scalded, burned, or trampled. He learns not to trip, for the lapse in bodily control is felt to leave him open to spirits that seek to possess him. Later in life, he might repeat various formulae before having intercourse, for sex also involves vulnerability through lessened control.

Children, of course, develop these survival skills over time, but it is particularly crucial that parents provide them with such protections during their early years, for at that time they are deemed especially vulnerable. Taroudannt women agree, for example, that small children are the most frequent victims of "the eye," with Moroccans occasionally explaining their high infant mortality rate in these terms. One mother extrapolated from her own tragic experience: her husband had bought a white robe for their five-year-old son for the holiday that comes at the close of Ramadan (l- 'id ṣ-ṣghir); the child wore it that day and appeared sublimely beautiful; that same day he was eyed in the street, and that evening he died. His mother said that he joined many others—more than half those in the cemetery—who had died in like fashion.

That same mother looked back and questioned her judgment in letting her son parade himself. In the old days, she said, not only virgins were kept hidden in order to protect them; small children were also kept dirty and disheveled in order to ward off "the eye." No rational human being, after all, would covet ugliness, and so "the eye" stopped automatically. Moroccans, of course, were aware that a child's unattractiveness might only be skin deep, and indeed might be a sign of a mother's particular concern and affection. Nonetheless, the technique left covetous desires automatically repulsed.

Similarly, children are especially vulnerable to evil spirits like the *tabe'*. The *tabe'* (literally "that which follows") haunts and debilitates luckless persons. The result might be death, illness, or a retardation of growth. A baby that does not crawl or talk probably has been struck by *tabe'*, according to belief. So, too, has the virgin who is competent and comely, but whose suitors reject her mysteriously. Some mothers see the tenacious desires of the *tabe'* as causing a child-raising period that is continuously harrowing. Mbiriku's mother gave her white daughter the name of a black woman in order that the child might gain the power of the blacks in the survival fight, for the mother had misgivings about the strength of her progeny: four prior babies had died. The name seemed to help only in a limited way, however, for Mbiriku later showed no inclination to walk. As a result, the mother dedicated her child at the yearly feast of a powerful brotherhood, again associated with the blacks *(l-'abid)*. The girl began attempting to walk that same day, the mother reported. The relief, however, seemed still incomplete, for Mbiriku was not snapped up in marriage after menarche, as were some other virgins. This time the mother resorted to other supernatural devices and had a curer fight the *tabe'* by cutting the daughter's cowlick. A suitor arrived some months later, and Mbiriku finally married. Only then did the mother feel that the *tabe'* had disappeared, and that she could finally rest. Significantly, Mbiriku's mother began calling her Mbaraka at that time, the more usual version of her name and one that has no black connotation.

Growing up in Taroudannt thus entails learning to use a repertoire of techniques for protection. During early childhood these mechanisms are many. Thereafter, their use tapers off as individuals age and gain strength. The birth *srira* falls off and is sometimes not replaced. The ill-kempt child of one or two years reaches age six or seven and is dressed cleanly and neatly. The adolescent all too often turns his back on the saints.

In keeping with the differentiation of male and female developmental pathways, the acquisition of these mechanisms and the
sloughing off of them has its own male-female dynamic. Both
boys and girls are believed to be born pure and naïve in spirit.
Thereafter, however, boys and girls are felt to move out of this
purity differentially. In particular, girls are felt to adopt protective
devices more quickly, completely, and tenaciously. They are said
to have *niya* (positive intention; good will) with respect to the
saints and those other supernatural forces that can provide them
with aid. By contrast, boys more frequently and cynically turn
their backs upon holy protectors. A young man's derangement or
illness, for example, is sometimes cited as being caused by his
foolhardiness vis-à-vis saints.

Taroudannt dwellers thus feel that boys exhibit a greater vulnerability than girls. Young girls are believed to steel themselves
more adequately against negative powers, a battle which they
fight all the more easily, because negative powers are felt to be
less attracted to them. This appraisal seems to range widely as an
Arab-Muslim perception: Lane (1908: 58), for example, reported
that nineteenth century Egyptian mothers believed that girls were
less open to envy ("the eye") and so disguised their sons by
dressing them in female clothing.

Ironically, the development of adult sexuality reintroduces anxiety about boys' safety just at the point at which fears of other
dangers come to be somewhat allayed. This renewed anxiety is
tied to what Mernissi (1975: 13) identifies as *fitna*, the Moroccan
term for chaos which also connotes a beautiful woman. *Fitna*
brings to mind the prostitute who is feared for her ability to hold
her lover otherwise impotent, a power that keeps men captive and
breaks marital bonds. It also recalls the animalistic Aisha Qandisha
figure, who hides her true ugliness—her hooves and her pendu-
lous breasts, for example—under dark hair, burning eyes, and
seductive robes. Aisha uses her superficial beauty to lure men in

the darkness, leading them to have intercourse with her and then tying them to her eternally. She robs them of success, intellect, and freedom, leaving them gutted of their better selves. Men who wander the streets aimlessly are sometimes called the lovers of Aisha. By contrast, no woman is believed to be led into a comparable state of oblivion by a mythical male sexual being.

Chaos, of course, is also brought about by other negative forces. *Tabe'* prevents marriage; the evil eye brings death and illness; Aisha Qandisha causes deviance; *jnun* bring the obliviousness that is evident in convulsions and trance. Each of these threatens the life force, contorts social life, and/or weakens social bonds.

Moroccan culture gears itself toward containing (and yet also maintaining) these chaotic tendencies. *Jnun* are repelled by a ṣrira and so are kept in the underworld; the evil eye is warded off by the showing of the five fingers of the hand; Aisha Qandisha is neutralized by the plunging of an iron knife into the ground; and women are kept at bay through their segregation and seclusion. The Taroudannt dweller feels that he or she should show constant vigilance in applying these remedies and in remembering these dangers, not least among them the last.

JUSTICE

Most Moroccans say that the separation of the sexes is necessary for the maintenance of order, if not harmony, in a basically hostile world. Why, however, are women "secluded" and not men; why are women limited to the smaller rather than the larger life-space? If Moroccans point to conceptions of order as one way of validating sex separation, they sometimes allude to notions of justice as one means of validating female seclusion, generally after the fact.

The need for order and the difficulty of providing justice form
two significant strands in the complex network of themes that
comprise Moroccan political philosophy. Depending largely upon
situational context Moroccans join these strands in varying ways.
"Sixty years of tyranny are better than one hour of civil strife"
says a long-standing and well-worn Islamic tradition which brings
together the two notions in a way that gives order priority. (It is a
tradition that Western scholarship has emphasized to the neglect
of counterthemes, as certain scholars [Asad 1974] remind us and
as I will show farther along.) According to it, the injustice caused
by one or a few persons holding power is less injurious than the
social injustice which would be caused by all upon all during a
period of anarchy. At the time of the abortive coup d'état attempt
in 1971, many Taroudannt dwellers expressed their fears in
essentially these terms. If the King had been killed, people would
probably have roamed the streets, killing, fighting, and stealing.
Insanity would have become the order of the day in the land. The
King's supporters would have neither eaten nor slept: these
excesses are natural responses when people experience grief. His
opponents, the victors, would also have avenged themselves
according to whim, taking whatever they fancied. Whichever
group emerged victorious, both sides would have lived
uncontrolled.

According to this view, stern, continuing order works to justice's
benefit not because justice thrives in order's presence but rather
because injustice is apt to be even more marked in periods of
upheaval. Justice, like virtue, remains an elusive quantity. The
Taroudannt tales underscore this pessimism, implying the short-
comings of even peaceful reigns, and further allude to some
reasons for these failings. Power and wealth, they imply, provide
rulers, real or potential, with an environment that is hostile to the
easy development of morality and responsibility, particularly if
those rulers have tasted power for a time. The ruler, coddled,

humored, aided, and feared from the moment of his birth, has little occasion to experience the adversity which provides one important context for attaining the responsibility that just rulers need.

Given this frame of reference, it is logical that people will expect the sultan, the police commissioner, and the judge (who are all men) to seek to maximize their own pleasures. Money, power, and the leisure that the umbrella of authority affords attract and seduce the political personage. The following two tales reflect people's expectations in the face of it: their finely honed cynicism concerning wielders of power.

Tale 29: The Judge

There once was a judge who was bothered by the many people who came to him for judgments. So he told his guards to soap all the steps leading to his courtroom. As a result, all fell down the stairs when they started up to his chamber, and no one ever reached him. Finally, the Prophet was told of this calamity. As punishment, he transformed the judge, making him a crow in the sky.

Tale 30: The Greedy Judge

A man left his wife and two children and went off to work in another country. Two years later, he came back, to find his wife with four children. "Whose are these last two children?" he asked. "They are yours; they are Hmed and Hussein," she answered. "It is not possible," he responded and decided to take his grievance to court.

The wife guessed at his plan and developed her own response to it. She took some plaster, cut it into rounds, and painted them like money. Then she put them into a pouch. When the husband took his wife to court, she stood at a safe distance behind him and showed the judge the moneybag. When the judge saw it, he berated the husband: "You left your wife pregnant, and these children are yours. Go, care for them."

On the way home from the court, the husband carried one child on his back and took the other by the hand. And when he met people on the road, he said to them with sarcasm, "If you want children, go to the court. The judge is doling out whore's children." As to the judge, he gained the pouch and quickly discovered the deception, but the woman had already gone off.

Given a bent toward injustice among those who are born to power, it is not surprising that the best of sultans and judges in the Taroudannt tales are those who have been subjected to hardship, men who were reared in poverty and who largely by virtue of it attained a measure of wisdom. These men sometimes bring a taste of justice to their reigns as they install themselves within a power system which they have not learned to corrupt.

Tale 31: The King of the Cemetery

A man entered the town marketplace. There he found that watermelons were selling for one penny each. After leaving the town walls, he found that they were selling for one penny a basketful (of ten or so). Thereupon he decided that watermelon selling would be a good business. So he bought a basketful outside and proceeded to market.

At the gate to the city, however, the guard demanded one as his pay. So did the supervisor of the market. Thereafter another two were taken for the Sultan, two for his minister, and three for the qaid. Finally, only one melon was left. The man sold that melon for one penny and realized no profit.

Said the man, "If this is how the city is run, then I will find another place, for there is no justice in it." And so he went to the cemetery to sit and to think. While he was thinking, a burial procession arrived and he charged it one penny. For each person who died, he asked a penny, and people met his demand. With time, he became known as the King of the Cemetery.

One day, the daughter of the qaid died and was taken to be buried. The man asked her mourners to pay. "It is the daughter of the qaid," they said with amazement. "Even if it is the daughter of the Sultan, the penny must be paid." The mourners of the *qaid's* daughter pondered and then paid it.

A while later, the son of the Sultan died, and they brought him to the cemetery. To them also the King of the Cemetery said, "Pay." The mourners refused, however, and reported back to the Sultan. "Which *qaid* put that man in the cemetery?" he asked. "He has been there as long as we can remember," they answered. The Sultan responded: "Then bring him to me."

The King of the Cemetery met the Sultan and explained that the city had no justice. He then recounted the story of the watermelons. Said the Sultan, "If you can rule more justly, I will make you King of the Market, but first instruct me what is to be done." To this, the King of the Cemetery said that anyone caught in the marketplace after sunset should be beheaded. Then in order to assure the legality of the measure, he drew up a contract and had the Sultan sign it.

From that day on, the market ran smoothly. People sold until nightfall and then left for their homes. No one passed in the streets of the marketplace after hours, and there was no theft.

After a number of months, the Sultan decided to visit the marketplace, for he had heard that justice had come to reign within it. So one evening, he strolled there with his wives. He found that the stores were left open and yet lacked for nothing, and he was truly astonished, for there was order and peace. Suddenly, however, the King of the Market appeared. He ordered his police to seize the Sultan and his women. Showing the Sultan the contract, the King of the Market had the ruler beheaded. Then he had himself crowned as the new Sultan and took over the former Sultan's wives.

The tale of the King of the Cemetery reveals a countertheme or qualifier to the "sixty years of tyranny" stance: the notion that rebellion or revolution might encourage justice, particularly if such action brings outsiders to power. And yet the ephemerality of justice still remains, a view that was much emphasized by the political philosopher Ibn Khaldun (Mahdi 1964), himself a North African. Virtually all rulers are corruptible. And should a new ruler prove to be just, his heirs are less likely to be responsible. Thus while rebellion or revolution might provide a temporary reprieve from oppression, the political pendulum almost assuredly swings back. Pessimism and cynicism emerge as wholly appropriate responses in the light of these perceptions.

WOMEN AND PUBLIC POWER

The callousness and egotism that Moroccans impute to most rulers and their underlings are felt to elicit varying responses from women. Some women use the waywardness of the powerful for their own ends. Other women are outraged by the male ruler's depravity and challenge it, thereby revealing their social responsibility and wisdom. Those women exert another positive influence upon the nexus of political power, but like the political reformer who seizes power from the outside, their justice is also deemed fleeting.

Tale 32: The Box

There once was a judge who married a young women whom he valued highly. One day he swore that if ever they separated, she could take the one thing that she most desired. He promised this out of affection.

And that judge did not judge fairly, which angered his wife. Hearing him give decisions always in favor of those who paid him best, she went to the window and repeated his transactions to passersby. Soon the people complained of the judge's corruption, and the judge deduced that the traitor must be his wife. He ordered her out of his house, telling her to take the one thing that she most valued as the promised gift from him.

But the wife had taken precautions. Days before, she had summoned a carpenter and had ordered him to craft a large wooden box. When her husband asked what it was that she wanted, she pointed to the box and answered: "It is you that I want. Here is a box. Climb into it." The judge stepped in as she had commanded, and then his wife locked it. Soon he begged for his freedom and obtained it, but only with the understanding that he would rule justly in her company and would never try to leave her again.

Tellers of the tale explain that the judge's wife was young, still at the age of not having borne children. By contrast, for most older women, the pendulum of justice is seen to swing back, and women are portrayed as exerting a strongly negative political influence. The effects of this shift are reflected in the following tale in which a woman misguides her husband, a prophet, in life-and-death policy affairs.

Tale 33: Saint Sulaiman

Saint Sulaiman, the prophet, ruled over all the feathered animals, the animals with poison, and the beings of the underworld. And he had a wife. First, she asked for pillows filled with wool and he brought them to her. Then she asked for pillows filled with cotton and he brought them to her. Then she asked for pillows filled with the feathers of birds. And he summoned all the birds of the world in order to fulfill her wishes. Some left eggs in their nests; some left fledglings without food. For three days they gathered. On the third day, the owl finally appeared. Saint Sulaiman scolded the owl, saying, "Why have you dallied?" The owl answered, "I was measuring. First, I measured to see if the night equaled the day, and I thought that it did. But then I thought again and saw that the day was more than the night, for the night was half day: it had the moon in it. Then I measured to see if the number of women equaled the number of men, and I thought that it did. But then I thought again and I saw that there were more women than men, for half the men of the world were really women: they did all that their women requested." And Saint Sulaiman understood, and sent all the birds back, with the owl as judge over all of them, for he measured well. (Indeed, the owl saved Saint Sulaiman from a multitude of sins, the sins done to the birds that he planned to defeather, for all surely would have died.) As to his wife, the prophet divorced her.

How probable is it that a woman might avert the depravity that Saint Suleiman's wife exhibits and so become a judicious ruler for the better part of her life? Although the tale of the box underscores the possibility, more general developmental premises imply that the likelihood is slight. Men are said to shift their concern from self to family to Allah, while women are propelled in the opposite direction: irresponsibility joins lasciviousness in a woman's later years. One Taroudannt folktale reifies this sequence as social "history": it portrays the south of Morocco as initially matriarchal, with the shift toward patriarchy resulting from women's misuse of power.

Tale 34: The Women of the Market

At the time of Adam and Eve, or shortly thereafter, women ruled the earth. In particular, they controlled the marketplaces, where they bought, sold, and traded. They also contracted marriages at will and divorced as they liked. Then, unlike men, who continued to go briefly to market, women began to go to the marketplace from morning to night. They also began to marry by whim and let jealousy disrupt their marriages. Allah therefore decreed that men should have authority over women, since women's rule had become excessive. (Women were taking nine, ten, eleven husbands at the time of this change.)

ENLIGHTENED DESPOTISM

When one looks at the future in probabilistic terms, as Moroccans appraise them, the concentration of authority in men's hands has its advantages. Nonetheless, the overall political prognosis remains rather despairing, for wise rulers are deemed few whether they be males or females, and those citizens who deal with them are seen as likely to emerge injured and maligned. The wrath of the unjust ruler is apt to oppress them: they are likely to be punished through royal egotism, cheated in the marketplace, and self-servingly dispatched by a judge or *qaḍi*. The Sultan finds the peasant's gift of figs to be disrespectful (tale 12); the *imam* has the pious woodcutter mistakenly arrested (tale 4); the judge takes the bribe of the wife of the cuckolded worker in the child support case (tale 30).

The suffering that this injustice entails is most immediately the suffering of men, for men comprise that portion of the populace that deals directly with the outside political world. By contrast, women are discouraged from taking part in public political transactions, a fact of life which Moroccans sometimes assert works to women's advantage. This conclusion is implicit, for example, in the tale of the quince (tale 12): the father is punished for both himself and his daughter, who suffers no penalty although she helped shape his gift-giving plan.

Removal from the outside world could not be depicted as advantageous to women, of course, if injustice were seen as equally apt to occur in the narrower sphere of the family as in the polity. Rather life in the household emerges as preferable, because injustice is felt to occur differentially, with responsibility and morality more frequently characterizing family power relations. The self-serving actions of men who hold public authority thus contrasts with what are depicted as the often more responsible deeds of men who hold household authority, as the tale of the box (tale 32) indicates. Men who have authority in the family, the tales imply, tend to reward women when women's behavior is good (tales 16, 20), in addition to punishing women when their behavior merits punishment (tales 8, 25, 27). And men are prone not merely to punish their wives, sisters, and daughters; they also show compassion, educate, and forgive (tales 28, 35). The following tale culminates with a display of this kind of magnanimity.

Tale 35: The Harvest

There once were a man and his wife, and he was a farmer. When the time of the harvest came, he realized a harvest that was bountiful, a harvest that when threshed left a pile of barley so high that no one could see over it. One day the wife's mother came to visit. At mid-morning she accompanied her daughter out to the threshing floor in order to bring the farmer his meal. Said the daughter to her mother as they stood before the grain pile, "Look at the bounty that Allah has accorded us." Then telling her mother to stand on one side of the pile, she went to the other side and repeated, "See, the pile is so high that you cannot even see me. There certainly is enough here for two or three years."

The two women returned to the house. There the mother suddenly interjected: "So much bounty. With what is left your husband surely will take a second wife. Here, then, is how you prevent this. Only you and he have the key to the storehouse. Every time I visit, you must give me a measure of barley, and I will take it home to store it. That way you will have your fair share of the abundance, and your husband's surplus will be gone."

The husband, however, overheard the women and decided to teach them. Each time the wife removed a measure for her mother, he took two measures and stored it with his friend. In six months the grain of three years was gone.

When the barley was depleted, the husband approached his wife. "Where has it gone?" he asked her. "There was enough there for two or three years." The wife gave no answer. Then he added, "You must replace it so that we can eat through the year." With that, she gave him her silver brooches for grain. Then she sold her silver bracelets and belt. Each time the husband took the jewelry to his friend and returned with some of the grain that he had secretly stored. By the end of the year, she had given over all her jewelry, clothing, and fine furnishings in order to get food for the household.

Soon the time of the next harvest came, and the mother again returned to her daughter. This time the daughter said angrily, "See what you have done. All my clothing and jewelry are gone." The wife's mother looked and then said resolutely: "I will take some of this year's grain and sell it for you. Then you can buy back your finery and goods." "No," said the wife. "You will not take one grain of barley; it is you who worked this misery upon me. If my husband marries ten times over, not one grain of barley will I take from him."

With that, the husband knew that his wife had learned. Little by little, he gave back her jewelry, fine clothing, and household goods as presents, and the two lived content.

The belief that justice is more likely to exist in the family sphere
is consistent with the developmental dynamic that is ascribed to
men's lives, for in their outward movement from self to family to
the community to Allah, men are said to pass the initial stage
rather easily but to add the later stages only through considerable
effort. As one old devout put it, "First one wins the blessing of
one's parents. Then one wins the blessing of the *shex* (brotherhood leader). Finally, one attains the blessing of Allah." The latter
blessings come with age, if at all.

For the most part, the particular combination of ideas that
Moroccan men and women hold about politics, power, and
authority further enmesh both sexes in a system of male domination and female subordination. In a variety of ways women learn,
through men and also through women, that women do well to
limit their interactions to the family sphere. Restriction and repres-
sion as such do not comprise the dominant connotations of
female seclusion: rather the practice comes to be viewed as one
that promotes women's personal well-being. Concurrently, men
are not seen as benefiting from the freedoms that they hold:
instead they sustain burdensome responsibilities. According to
one appraisal (Rosenfeld 1960), the Arab-Muslim women of Israel
apply a similar political model in their kin relations, opting for what
Westerners might describe as dependency but what those women
and their men might more readily call enhanced protection. They
assert that they have consciously abdicated certain of their freedoms in an attempt to attain security. The trade-off, as phrased by
Moroccan women's Arab-Israeli sisters, is deemed a good one by
both sides.

Chapter Eight
VARIATIONS ON A THEME

Let us return to the women as they speak to other women and what they say of their men. There is Sultana, whose husband occasionally had intercourse with prostitutes and whose babies died as a consequence, or so she believed. Sultana's women friends urged her to ask him to wash more thoroughly so that the infants would not succumb to the smell of sex on him, rather than advising her to insist upon his faithfulness. Their words ultimately rested upon the hard reality that Sultana did not have the power to constrain her husband's behavior but were also forwarded along broader lines, namely that sexual wandering is what "men do." Her husband, for his part, described his visits in other terms: he felt that prostitutes offered him a service which he bought or refused as the result of rational decision-making. A second instance concerns Fatima, whose husband first drank alcohol while working with the Jews and who later came to squander his

149

money illegally on European drink (drinking is prohibited by Islam). Her three-year-old son walked by one day, clutching an empty liquor bottle, listing to and fro in his baby walk. Said Fatima wryly, "Men are all alike," at the same time expressing her doubts that any son of her husband would ever be likely to support her. Fatima's husband, by contrast, talked of his life with pride, citing his recent involvement with an important religious brotherhood as the proper priority in his life. And finally, there is the case of Miriam, the wife of the aged devout, whose guidelines for godly living have already been mentioned, among them being the limitation of sexual relations to once a half-month. Miriam did not deny that sexual moderation was appropriate to the religious life; rather she questioned cause and effect, and called into doubt the motivation behind her husband's newly cultivated stance. Her husband, like many men, took on the brotherhood devotion and performed the pilgrimage to Mecca, she said, only when he evinced a lessened competence at sex.

In addition to the more generalized framework which men and women hold regarding male and female proclivities, there are certain divergences in beliefs and attitudes about men and women, as offered by the two sexes. Cynicism and pessimism pervade much of the belief system that both men and women hold, but the bite of cynicism is especially marked among women, for it occurs not only as women talk of women in stereotypic terms, but also as women talk of their men. Women's greater cynicism regarding men focuses upon the improbability of men attaining the total wisdom and control that define the last stage of the male developmental trajectory. That likelihood is sufficiently reduced in women's eyes so as to drop the average man to a low level in most women's estimation. Unlike men, who sustain greater hopes for good performance from the male sex, women voice strong doubts about the average man's behavior in the major realms of social life. Their scathing criticism of men as a category joins their scathing criticism of women, and thereby opposes itself to the more narrowly channeled criticism which men direct particularly at women, as they depict the two sexes' performances in sexual, familial, and extrafamilial affairs.

VIEWS ON ADULT SEXUALITY

Moroccan men commonly impute uncontrolled passion to their adult women. Some call women "cows" because of their putative animality. Many say women share their brains with donkeys, a reference not only to the donkey's stupidity but also to the female's recognition of the male animal's marked genital endowment. Indeed, men imply that the female of whatever species has an insatiable desire to be penetrated. Although the plowman eventually tires, states one metaphor, the land (womankind) continues to await his plow with undiminished eagerness.

The stereotype of uncontrolled female passion is held not only by men. Women also call upon it in characterizing women. Women are like baskets, said one mother-in-law with reference to her daughter-in-law's unflagging sexual interest: as with baskets, women's bottoms (their genitals) form their most essential parts; as with baskets, women are conceived of as useless without them.

While characterizing other women in terms of heightened passion, Taroudannt women typically tend to be more charitable in their self-characterizations. Most say that they can control and channel their sexual impulses. Even in their own cases, however, they do not generally challenge the more fundamental belief about intense female passion. Rather, they emphasize their own unusual self-control as the element that holds a powerful female sexuality in check.

Because women, like men, subscribe to the image of raging female passion, men's and women's conceptions of female sexuality do not differ perceptibly with regard to this most basic element. Rather, differences in sexual beliefs become evident when the two sexes enumerate and describe the attributes of maleness. For their part, men tend to see satiability as a basic element in their own sexual interactions. "What gets tired, the tunnel or the rat?" "What runs dry, the river or its bed?" Such aphorisms typically recounted by men, replete with the imagery of women's mindless passion, also convey the message of lessened drive and passion for the male sex.

Women, however, do not typically allude to satiability when describing male behavior. Instead they view men as possessing their own quotient of insatiability and waywardness. "A man is like the hands of a clock, he (his penis) points in all directions," one women asserted regarding men's sexual loyalties and interest. In a similar vein, another woman affirmed "a man is like the river; he cuts his bed in one place one year and in another the next." Women see little nobility, restraint, or logic impelling men's sexual relations. If women are animal and so can rightfully be denigrated, men also are animal and so merit condemnation, although this disapproval must be guardedly expressed (Vinogradov 1974: 196).

The difference between the two sexes' conceptions of maleness is particularly apparent in their opposing representations of two core concepts, *'aqel* and *nifs*. Men expound the view that they especially have or can develop more *'aqel* (intelligence, responsibility, rationality) while women have more *nifs* (flesh-centered desires and tensions). Derogatory and rather obscene in its usage, the term *nifs* is sometimes used by men in referring to their own baser instincts but is more generally used to portray the propensities of women. Women utilize it less frequently, but when they do, it is often in a similar fashion: they employ the concept when characterizing other women's sexuality. Here again, women promote an image of women which focuses upon animal characteristics. As importantly, however, women also extend the notion of *nifs* to their characterizations of men. "They [men] say that we have more *nifs* [than men do]," is a frequent female response to the question of whether women really have more *nifs* and less *'aqel*. Women then generally proceed to express doubts about the lesser animality of men. Interestingly, one woman interpreted *nifs* as emotionality in the sense of sensitivity of soul, especially as it concerns interpersonal relations within the nuclear family. Having defined it in that way, she readily agreed that women have more of it.

At issue, then, is not the belief that women are passionate and animalistic, a fact of life with which women heartily agree, but rather the assertion that men are less so than women. Men, in women's eyes, can be consumed with desire of a sexual sort, and can be shamefully profligate, quite like the female sex according to the male view.

As might be expected, of course, women do not air their views before men, women, and outsiders to the same degree that men verbalize their beliefs. In keeping with their more precarious position in Moroccan society, women are guarded in expressing their attitudes, and generally limit their pronouncements about men to exchanges with persons of their own sex. On these all-female occasions, however, women often emphasize the lowered male image. They often call male sexuality and intelligence into question, and laugh together at men who run after women and so show their foolishness. Indeed, while women often point to women's animality before other women through comments like "women's minds are in their vulvas," they as often extend the allusion to men by asserting that "men's minds are in their penises."

Given the derogatory image that women put forth about men, it is not surprising that modesty *(ḥeshma)* is not the only female quality that women laud. Almost as important in women's eyes is patience *(ṣber)*. Indeed, while men and women alike stress modesty heavily in evaluating women's behavior, women also stress patience as a female behavioral ideal. Again, these different emphases get to the heart of differing male and female attitudes about the two sexes: while both sexes stress female frailties and so seek to counteract them through an emphasis upon modesty, women also recognize the existence of male frailties and so feel that women must steel themselves against these disruptive influences through patience.

Despite women's rather cynical view of male fidelity, disgrace, in both women and men's eyes, still falls upon women and not men for engaging in sexually illicit liaisons. No matter how demanding the man, it is the woman who must stand firm against him or who, by submitting, must ultimately pay the social price. Ironically, this view is especially tenacious, for both men's and women's ideologies can and do accommodate the assertion. In the male view, women take on the role of temptress and are considered more profligate. From women's perspective, women know men to be wayward and dissolute, and so little tolerance is shown to women when they assert that men have seduced them. For women, ignorance or innocence provide no viable excuses for girls or women who submit to premarital or extramarital sex.

VIEWS ON PARENTHOOD

Portrayals of fathers and mothers emerge logically given the views of male and female sexuality that men and women hold. Men see women as capable of sacrificing their children for sex, for they see women as strongly sexually motivated. By contrast, men view themselves as providing a measure of rationality in parent-child relations, a rationality which is consistent with the male self-image of sexual balance. Women, for their part, see men as being sharply limited in their parental feelings and loyalties, for they see men's innate sexual tendencies as competing with their paternal tendencies. In keeping with women's somewhat negative self-image, however, they also recognize the possibility, although not the likelihood, of their own parental weakness.

The correspondence of the sexual and parental images remains incomplete, it must be stressed, because of the nature of women's maternal self-image. Whereas women's belief in their own powerful sexuality might imply a negative valuation of their maternal tendencies, maternity, in fact, generally carries a strong positive valuation among Moroccan women. Women definitely view themselves as the caring ones in situations of child rearing. And yet, and quite importantly, I would argue, that positive image remains incomplete: a belief in mother's potential treachery continues to exist.

The Moroccan legal system recognizes this tension between women's sexuality and maternity, and in effect makes it one basis for imposing limitations upon women's rights and privileges regarding children. Mothers are felt to be the physiologically appropriate rearers of their children, and so guardianship is normally accorded to them or to other female relatives in the event of a couple's divorce. The law deems those same mothers to be fit for the guardian role, however, only when they restrict their sexual desires by eschewing outside sexual involvements and by rejecting subsequent marriages. Their sexuality, when actualized, is felt to work to parenthood's loss. Mothers thus lose their guardianship at the time of remarriage, according to statute. It is felt that through a desire to please a new husband and through a need for sexual satisfaction, a woman will slight even her own daughter or son.

An ideological document that is totally the creation of men, the Moroccan legal code understandably reflects men's attitudes about sexuality and parenthood. It is thus not surprising that the code accords with basic male notions about a mother's potential for treachery. It is also not surprising that the code is more generous in its treatment of men. The father who has guardianship over his children and then remarries, for example, retains control over his children. While female sexuality and maternity work at cross-purposes according to the male perspective, fatherhood and male sexuality are not necessarily regarded as conflicting.

If men's perceptions are institutionalized in the Moroccan legal code, women's perceptions are institutionalized in what women believe the legal code contains. These beliefs are significant in that women gear their lives to them, being unaware that their beliefs often do not accord with statute. Thus women believe that women will remain sexually pure when in the presence of children, and many assume that the code reflects this belief. They often state that the presence of a child provides them with legally recognized protection for their reputations when they venture out alone. When children accompany them, women feel that their husbands have no moral or legal right to divorce them for dalliance.

From the ideological vantage, women's beliefs about these protections are in keeping with women's perceptions about sexuality and parenthood. Ultimately, they hinge upon women's faith in the strength of their maternal feelings. Few women, say women, would commit immoralities in the presence of their children. This feeling is so strong, say women, that the tendency is operative even if the child is not yet aware, if it is still a babe in arms.

The same folk beliefs, however, also allow for the possibility of mother's betrayal and so are not totally laudatory to women. From women's commentary, for example, it is clear that the maternal instinct has precedence over sexual desire when the two are placed in direct confrontation. When a direct confrontation of stimuli is lacking, however, women are felt capable of neglecting their children, leaving them untended in order to engage in extramarital sex.

The female view of maternal loyalty, then, is conditional, whereas the male view involves unconditional distrust. In a like manner, while men see their paternal impulses in a generally positive light, women tend to view paternal feelings with extreme skepticism. Women say that their own *kibda* (liver or "heart" in our sense) is given over to children while men's *kibda* is devoted to business, same-sexed peers, and other women. From the female viewpoint, paternity plays only a minor role in male motivation, and so male sexuality is seen inevitably to win out in the battle of parenthood and sex. Women see this outcome as consistent with physiological and social realities. Women argue: a woman carries her child during pregnancy, then she carries it on her back for several years; finally she raises it. How can a father equal the closeness that such continued contact affects?

VIEWS ON EXTRAFAMILIAL INTERACTIONS

With regard to the wider world beyond the family, much as with regard to family life itself, Moroccans tend to evaluate the worth of men and women according to interactive criteria. One is seduced by or is faithful to; one is modest before or is brazen toward; one betrays or protects. Character does not emerge superordinately as a conglomerate of internal tendencies and feelings that sometimes reach external expression, as Americans, for example, are wont to conceptualize it; instead character exists to the extent to which it is interactively expressed.

It is thus not unexpected that male and female character, which are conceptualized as different in the Moroccan schema, are also conceived of as being expressed differently at the general interactive level, and that the two sexes, which hold differing views about male and female propensities for sexuality and parenthood, should also hold differing beliefs about the bases for different male and female styles of interaction. From the male point of view, this difference in male and female styles revolves around the progressive development of female stubbornness and egotism, a developmental tendency which they feel men do not share. From the female point of view, the difference between male and female styles is less prominent: women are felt to develop an exaggerated stubbornness, but men are also felt to display contentiousness and self-centeredness.

The negative interactive complex, which is particularly associated with women, can be subsumed under the cover term of *dela' 'awja* ("twisted rib" or "chest"), a general inability to make peace or compromise. If women fight, it is said, they will always continue fighting, and will never again come together in friendship. Moreover, if they form an opinion, whether out of love or in enmity, they will be subsequently closed-minded to others' opinions and views. Roudaniyin feel that women are prisoners of their hatreds, perpetuating them even when propriety, loyalty, and good sense demand conciliation.

Dela' 'awja rears its ugly head in family as well as in non-family matters. The following examples, provided by two women and one man, respectively, are illustrative of its form and effects:

1. The old Berber woman Yemena always begged for money, although her son, with whom she lived, had sufficient income to support her. Moreover, she tucked away her earnings instead of sharing them with her child. Upon her death, neighbors reported that a 100,000 *ryal* note ($1,000) was found hidden among her

possessions. Yemena was said to have ḍela' 'awja not so much because she took from outsiders under false pretenses but because of the effect that her begging had upon her son. He knew of her dissumulation and yet found that he could not berate his mother. He thus was forced to endure shame until and after her death.

2. Taja, mother of two middle-aged sons who worked their mother's land, had provided herself with a substantial income through personal supervision of her olive groves. With her income she should have helped her sons find brides, and yet she did not. Instead she constantly refused to help them marry, desiring their attentions for herself alone. As a result of her self-centeredness, she fought with her sons almost continuously. Taja was said by her neighbors to have ḍela' 'awja in her family relations.

3. The old woman Ftoma was said to have ḍela' 'awja because of the tensions she caused in the neighborhood. She fought constantly with the other women over what she interpreted as discourtesies to her. Although her husband attempted to gét her to forget and forgive (for her actions affected certain financial dealings), she seldom made peace.

Ḍela' 'awja refers to a pettiness which is socially disruptive because it nullifies existing rights and obligations. It especially refers to discord in ongoing relationships. Neighborhood, affinal, and parent-child relations are particularly prone to be affected by older women's dela' 'awja. With respect to newly married women, who are still young and whom people believe do not exhibit the tendency so markedly, the mother-in-law – daughter-in-law relationship particularly is felt to reveal its disruptive effects.

A corresponding belief is that women lack a more comprehensive positive virtue, that of niya (interest in others, willingness to please). Unlike dela' 'awja, niya relates to voluntaristic behavior rather than the fulfillment of obligations. Lacking niya in sufficient measure, women are believed to shiyik or be shiki: that is, to act overbearingly and preciously when others merit their attention or aid. Women who *shiyik,* for example, tend not to talk to others as they attempt to emphasize their exclusiveness; they eat meagerly at celebrations, implying the superiority of their own daily food; they do not fix tea for their fellow guests, implying that others should serve them instead.

Both sexes tend to agree that *ḍela' 'awja* and *shiki* are particularly found in women, and in older women in greatest measure, while *niya* is particularly lacking among them. Women, however, more often cite variations in individual behavior when ascribing these characteristics, and often exclude themselves from their generalizations. Furthermore, they frequently cast aspersions upon the superiority which men feel they hold in carrying out interpersonal affairs.

The situation that men most often cite in order to demonstrate their lesser susceptibility to *ḍela' 'awja* is the marketplace transaction. Men will argue with one another, they say, and then fix upon a price with a smile. Similarly, partners and co-workers might dispute deeply during the course of a day but then will patch up their differences, realizing that continued enmity would be detrimental to each party's business affairs. The marketplace necessitates rationality, and men style themselves masters within the marketing realm.

Women, however, regard men's analysis of marketplace behavior as narrow and unrevealing. They themselves, say women, are equally reasonable in marketplace transactions, being decorous when necessary and seeking a good price. Rather, women display their perversity and stubbornness largely in more intimate relationships. But then men, say women, can also show a similar perversity in those contexts. Frequently, they cannot forgive and forget. Indeed, the numerous cases in which men abandon their families or are unfaithful to their wives demonstrate the fickleness and vengefulness which men can exhibit. Moreover, the many cases in which men violate what women believe to be their innate legal rights provide yet other examples, in women's view, of men's unsatisfactory behavior in close interpersonal relationships.

THE POLITICS OF PROTEST

Broadly, then, there are significant divergences between men's and women's views of themselves and the other sex, when male and female are taken as generalized categories. Each sex provides different appraisals of the wholesomeness of men's and women's sexuality, sociality, and parentalism. Men see women as sexually dangerous, socially volatile, and ever suspect, even with regard to their powerful maternal commitment. Significantly, women see women in essentially the same terms, although they tend to temper their indictment. Men, by contrast, portray themselves in a more favorable light: they say that they are or can be sexually satiable, socially adept, and parentally caring. Women, however, question these virtues and doubt that men as a group can be best depicted in these terms.

These different assessments, of course, can have varying effects upon the acting out of a system of male dominance and female subordination. Men's emphasis, for example, easily accords with the numerous other validations that have already been described, and so men emerge as superior from both the developmental and non-developmental vantages. Women's views, when taken from this more synchronic perspective, however, more nearly offer a challenge to the inequality notion, for men tend to sink to women's level in women's estimation. What, then, is the effect of women's occasional disbelief in men, their cynicism and skepticism? To what degree do these beliefs encourage dissatisfaction among the women of Taroudannt?

Whereas the data relating to these issues might at first seem straightforward and unambiguous—women have engaged in no protest of an organized or overt kind in southern Morocco—the issue, in fact, is far more complex, for protest of a more covert, more personalized kind does take place. It manifests itself not in the form of revolutionary action or reform movements, however, but through discrete and carefully veiled acts of rebellion.

Some rebellious behavior concerns sorcery of what women would call a morally positive type. Wives frequently work sorcery upon their husbands, for women regard men's loyalties as ever uncertain. Thus, virtually all Taroudannt women burn herbs and spices in order to give their husbands a pleasant disposition and in order to restrict their husbands' sexual interest. Women generally see sorcery as a potent mechanism through which men can be rendered faithful to their wives. Indeed, the belief that men are prone to straying sexually is so widespread that mother-in-law and daughter-in-law occasionally unite against the common male enemy. Mothers-in-law sometimes teach their sons' brides sorcery techniques or permit them to use sorcery. These women believe that daughters-in-law's sorcery, when of this positive kind, strengthens the marital unions that mothers-in-law initially instigated through their choices of brides.

A second set of rebellious acts involves petty theft. Virtually all married women pilfer money or goods in the urban areas in southern Morocco. They take small change from their husbands' pockets and/or limited amounts of oil or grain from their husbands' storehouses. Then they hide the money underground or in kitchen utensils or have neighborhood women sell the produce in private transactions or in the local marketplace. Again this behavior, which men vehemently condemn and strongly punish, is considered appropriate and logical by women; women feel that these valuables give them a measure of security as well as the means for satisfying future material desires. Many women call it their "right."

A third sphere of veiled rebellion centers upon the messages that women inculcate during child rearing. Mothers believe that their husbands can easily be overcome by their sexual desires and/or by other nonmarital interests (e.g., business, male friendships). As a means of imparting wariness to their children, mothers thus tend to spread the message of father's fickleness within the family, unbeknown to men. Again, women feel that such behavior is appropriate and might be essential to their children's survival.

From a practical viewpoint, these acts of rebellion constitute especially potent courses of action for women because sex segregation provides such activities with considerable shelter. Men's separation from women in many contexts makes it rather difficult for them to supervise and regulate their women. Other women tend to take on the role of supervisor in men's absence, but these women occasionally show sympathy and understanding for women's problems and so sometimes provide women with a degree of leeway in their family affairs.

In keeping with differences in men's and women's beliefs, the two sexes respond quite differently to the phenomenon of sex segregation itself. Men state that women should be kept separate, for they deem women to be inferior beings. At the same time, they assert that men should spend time with other men, for men necessarily provide men with a social environment of an appropriate sort. Women, by contrast, voice various rationalizations for the same practice. On the one hand, they see women's potential waywardness as necessitating restraint. On the other hand, they tend to support men's avoidance of women because it removes men from their life-space and gives women a better opportunity for independence and covert defiance in family affairs.

Women thus use men's belief in men's immediate superiority to their own advantage. Their critical attitude, however, focuses most strongly upon the positive image that men hold of men. The more negative image of women which is held by the population at large continues modified in women's eyes but still largely unchallenged. It is this blending of images that is operationalized in various contexts, but is especially apparent in most courtroom affairs. The Moroccan legal code, like local customary law, sharply circumscribes women's life alternatives. In effect, it limits the social, sexual, and geographical maneuverability of women according to the wishes of the male head of household. And yet women typically express dissatisfaction with only certain aspects of this social reality. Women's objections tend to focus upon men's excessive privilege rather than upon the heavy restrictions that women endure.

Skepticism about male superiority thus leads Moroccan women to respond with defiance and anger to the privileges that men enjoy. Certain aspects of women's self-image, however, discourage those same women from requesting increased privileges and rights. In effect, the sum total of women's beliefs supports some subversive activities while militating against protest that is aimed at a general increase in women's life options. As a consequence, women's acts of protest have tended to remain individual and veiled.

Chapter Nine
CONCLUSION

In the West, there are two sexes: the "second sex" and, by implication, the first sex, with each being the "opposite sex" to the other. According to the division, the first sex is always the male one (de Beauvoir 1949): the ranking of male and female never alternates, with the two being opposite not only in the sense of complementarity but also because they are provided with ultimately opposed valuations. Both male and female are apt to define the male-female difference in terms of pluses and minuses or greater than's and lesser than's with respect to the incidence of certain valued traits (e.g., intelligence, forcefulness, rationality) (Martin and Voorhies 1975: 40 f.).

The paradigm provides what many Westerners regard as a natural first step in categorizing humankind. Significantly, however, numerous other peoples in the world do not accept it. Some see the distinction between two innately separate sexes as untenable. The Dogon of the Niger Bend region of Africa (Griaule 1947) feel that each person is born with a male and female element, a male soul laid upon or below a female soul, with one of those souls dominating the other. Circumcision or cliterodectomy then removes the weaker element and establishes a complete adult sexuality. Other societies reject a second notion, that of opposition. Early in the history of sex role studies, for example, Mead (1935) described the Arapesh, whose males and females perceived their own and the other sex as similar in predisposition and behavior. And if Western men and women hold similar stereotypes for the two sexes, men and women in many other societies do not. The male New Guineans of Mt. Hagen call women mere producers, while women see women as essential in economic affairs (Strathern 1972).

Moroccans draw their own distinctive conclusions on these basic issues. Whereas Dogon see a spiritual and biological overlapping of the sexes, at least at the initial stages of children's lives, and whereas Arapesh see a general concordance of male and female characters, Moroccans suggest that males and females have continuingly opposed developmental pathways and thereby hold male and female to be always fundamentally different. This opposition, which both men and women espouse although many of their other conceptualizations differ, is not a constant one of the predominant Euro-American sort, however, but rather changes over time, with moral rank ascending in one case and descending in the other.

Such differences in fundamental premises stand as first indicators of the great variability that occurs regarding beliefs about maleness and femaleness. As one moves from society to society, belief complexes about sexuality differ markedly in form and content as well as in their use as moral guides. One cannot overemphasize this variability, for it points to the need for considerable caution regarding the formulation and use of the many generalizations that have been forwarded about the structure and functioning of sexual ideologies generally. To the degree that certain interpretations have made universalistic claims, Moroccan sexual ideology offers a testing ground as well as ultimately a call for more particular formulations.

Numerous explanations, for example, have been forwarded to account for the wide-ranging occurrence of female subordination, among them women's lesser strength, women's involvement in child rearing, men's control over heavy weaponry, men's lower threshold of aggression, and the nearly worldwide influence of a Western imperialist system that subordinates women. One set of hypotheses requires especial attention in this volume, for it concerns the politics of sexual life and the symbolism associated with it. It looks sometimes to human physiology, sometimes to the structure of social life, and sometimes to the organization of cognition, and asserts that differences in male and female functioning provide a symbolic framework that encourages people to perceive women as naturally subordinate to men. Ortner (1974) asserts that women are universally associated with the pain, blood, and inconvenience of menstruation and childbirth, with these constituting natural encumbrances: hence women must be subordinated, for nature must be subdued. Women, she says, are also associated with animalistic social contexts, for they bear and care for children, those humans who are closest to animals in their mental and bodily functioning. In this instance, women must also be controlled by men, society's more completely socialized element. A parallel distinction between more and less "cultural" jobs is made by Rosaldo (1975), who sees life-giving and life-taking as the main perceived distinction between male and female functioning among the Ilongot of the Philippines. She links men's superior position among the Ilongot to their involvement in headhunting, which she says is volitional; while birthing is a rather automatic outgrowth of sex, which is instinctually generated. Women as life-givers thus emerge as less distinctively human and cultural than men and thereby to be subdued. Ortner (1974) and S. Ardener (1975) and E. Ardener (1972; 1975) carry the female-nature association to yet another level, for they see women as socially and physically embedded in a world that is natural and concrete and that thereby does not encourage the creation and application of more abstract models, whether of social roles (Ortner 1974, using Chodorow 1974 and others) or of the encompassing world (E. Ardener 1972). Women, in turn, come to be associated with symbolic representations that are "less cultural" than men's.

Hypotheses that designate women's association with nature as underlying women's political position are not new to these times. Already in the mid-1800s, Bachofen (1967) noted that many societies link women symbolically to nature through the demands of the mother role. For Bachofen, however, this did not necessarily lead to women's subordination, but rather to variable power and authority depending upon how the female-mother-nature association is phrased and how it integrates with other beliefs. Female dominance, as exhibited in matriarchy, he affirmed, thus rested upon the symbolic "domination of the generative womb" (1967: 97), while male dominance as exhibited in patriarchy emerged when men added the notion of the father as linked to spirituality (1967: 109).

Implicit in the Bachofen stance is a realization that any observer must go beyond the search for atomistic root causes for women's status vis-à-vis men and must examine belief (and behavioral) complexes in which components are multivalent and intertwine. Since male-female relations constitute a highly complex behavioral sphere and since humankind naturally displays contemplative tendencies, it is logical to assume that the belief systems

associated with male-female relations, particularly in so fundamental an aspect as power distribution between the sexes, will be
elaborate. The data presented in this volume point to the validity
of this premise for the Moroccan case and the more general Arab-
Muslim one.

BLOOD, BIRTH, AND CHILD REARING

There is, for example, a complex set of Moroccan beliefs regarding pollution through blood and an associated lessening of
women's freedoms. For the Moroccan case it is certainly true that
the blood of menstruation and childbirth occasions numerous
restrictions upon women's activities. Religious devotions—prayer,
fasting, entering saintly tombs and mosques, even touching the
Koran—are all forbidden to the menstruating woman, for in that
state she is defiling. Some Roudaniyin say that her mere presence
in a mosque requires that it be torn asunder, bit by bit, and
cleansed, and the worshippers caught within it must all attend to
their own purification. Yet according to popular belief, semen is
also defiling in quite similar ways (see Faithorn 1975 for a descrip-
tion of a similar set of beliefs among the Kafe of Highland New
Guinea). Ejaculation renders men unfit to pray, fast, or enter
saintly shrines or mosques. Indeed, the cleansing process that
women undergo after their menstrual periods must be undertaken
after ejaculation. And if menstrual blood is believed to cause
illness (e.g., syphilis) in those men who are in contact with it
during intercourse, semen, when inappropriately handled, is also
believed to cause death and disease, as is aptly revealed in the
woman Sultana's bitterness toward her husband concerning the
deaths of her children (p. 149).

Thus while blood spells danger, so, too, does semen. Indeed, Moroccans tend to regard most bodily fluids as potentially dangerous. Blood-letting is believed to release harmful body juices and so remains a common first step in curing. Sweating is a primary goal of the public bath regimen: sweat must be exuded if one is to render oneself truly clean. Mucous is allowed to run freely from the nasal passages in children: there is a felt danger in its retention. A simple correlation between menstrual blood, danger, and female subordination thus takes its place within a broader conceptual schema relating to the dangers of bodily secretions and the need for men, women, and children consciously to control them.

Likewise, while childbearing defines the close association of women with babies, which are not-yet-human entities (beings without 'aqel, as Moroccans would call them), this is not an essentially negative association for Moroccans. Indeed, the Moroccan material implies a bit of the opposite (a view of women as enculturator which Ortner [1974: 79] characterizes as a logical alternative), for women are believed to display social responsiveness during pregnancy, parturition, and thereafter for variable time periods. In fact, women who die in childbirth die laudably, much as do soldiers engaged in the holy war. Both life-giving and life-taking are religious sanctioned, socially responsive, and necessary activities in these cases, and reflect positively upon men and women alike.

And yet it must not be forgotten that the life-giving enterprise, which emerges as essentially positive in the Moroccan case, is only one part of the maternal representation as Moroccans formulate it. Maternity is a variegated notion that implies both glories and insufficiencies which in their very contrastiveness comment upon women's position in the real world. In particular, it provides the promise of a quintessential givingness while simultaneously embodying the threat of betrayal. Moroccans do not represent motherhood as an unfailingly positive role ("the mother . . . as friendly, supportive, and generally admirable" as Friedl [1975: 68] describes the attitude for most patrilineal societies); nor do they view women in their roles as wives or sexual beings as "at best of doubtful loyalty, at worst as hostile, recalcitrant" (Friedl 1975: 68). Rather the maternal and sexual images are well-textured projections which conjoin complexly and which elicit a broad range of emotions regarding the women who undertake them.

Indeed, the Moroccan representation of the mother, if not the father, takes on a somewhat Freudian aspect through the particular mix of conflicting emotions that it evokes. There is filial love joined to the fear of mother's sexual infidelity. In the Moroccan case, however, the child's anxiety over the mother's seduction does not coalesce so strongly around the father, who is rarely an emotional rival, but rather is directed toward a more dangerous mind-figure, the outside male as lover, who is regarded as likely to trap the mother, seeking as she does sexual release, into betrayal.

THE DEVELOPMENTAL DYNAMIC

The nature of Moroccan family life, with its arranged marriages and easy divorces, would seem to encourage a thrust for betterment at the projective level, for most women and many men experience sexual dissatisfaction maritally, and Moroccans see both men and women as instinctually inclined to remedy the frustration, for they regard sex as a basic human drive. They thus recognize a continuing vector force for change, one which, in fact, is often actualized behaviorally: it sometimes exists under the cover of marriage, while at other times bringing about marriage's demise. A substantial number of women (and men), for example, engage in a limited sexual rebellion through their occasional involvement in illicit sexual affairs.

One can conjecture variously about the stimulus for the Taroudannt ideology's developmental thrust, whether it be a projection of fears generated in the family because of the fragility of parental relations, or whether it has its roots in phenomena that are less specifically Moroccan, such as the nature of sexuality itself. One can, for example, correlate certain aspects of the Moroccan male-female developmental dynamic with the changing shape of male and female sexual drives, at least to the extent that Western researchers have been able to gauge them. While United States' data on sexual involvement, expression, and potency for males and females at different stages in their life-spans can in no way be taken as proof of universal physiological tendencies, the isomorphism between certain statistical findings (Katchadourian and Lunde 1975: 190–93) and the Moroccan projective model is striking. According to both, men peak in their sexual involvement after puberty and in early adulthood and thereafter show a decline in intensity of sexual expression, while women involve themselves slowly, peak relatively late (in their thirties), and then show a slow decline.

Whether or not social life and/or physiology form crucial springboards for Moroccans' tendency to portray maleness and femaleness in developmental terms, one can certainly also attribute this preoccupation to a natural involvement with temporality generally. Human beings age, all the while reorienting their needs, desires, wisdoms, powers, and vulnerabilities, and the Taroudannt belief system reveals the society's concern with this process. Indeed, the Moroccan focus upon development is less to be explained than the relative paucity of developmental emphases in Western, especially American, thinking. De Beauvoir (1970) once commented bitterly that old age occasioned no serious recognition in the Western world, and one might also add that childhood, despite the continuing concern with it, often does not receive sufficient acknowledgment in the sense that it, too, is all too frequently portrayed as antithetical to adulthood. In particular, neither is deemed sexual, so that many of the powerful moments of human sexual development that occur during these life stages are obscured or lost.

Western anthropologists have moved cautiously beyond the basic premises of their culture's perceptual models as they seek to describe and discuss other peoples' perceptions of the life process. The renewed focus upon men's and women's life crises (Silverman 1967) surely constitutes a recent breakthrough in the shift away from more static models, much as the growing concern with middle and old age has helped redress the balance from Western society's disproportionate emphasis upon adult youth. Studies like the Silverman one, which designates life crises as points to be determined rather than as obvious and given, show that even seemingly inconsequential events in a life-span might be culturally designated as developmental benchmarks, while other seemingly momentous events or periods might be left unelaborated. (Mead [1928] demonstrated this early in relation to the lack of trauma regarding adolescence among the Samoans.) Furthermore, life crises must also be regarded contextually, for they often gain in significance through the manner in which they integrate into a continuing life stream.

Moroccans' almost total neglect of menarche as a turning point in female character development is a good case in point. Menarche is uncelebrated, essentially unacknowledged, and scarcely discussed among Roudaniyin. It is the rare Taroudannt woman who remembers the occurrence of any ritual behavior at the onset of her menstruation; in those few cases, the ritual was structurally sparse and is now defunct. Indeed, only one old woman remembered any public acknowledgment: a newly menstruating girl was told to climb her house's main staircase, eating dates and drinking milk as she then descended, step by step. Whatever the ritual, however, it remains rare in the Taroudannt case, for most girls hide the fact that they have begun menstruating from their mothers and other kinswomen, at least during the first months, for they regard menstruation with embarrassment.

Menarche, like circumcision, marks the attainment of a certain level of preparedness, but, much like circumcision, it is ignored in favor of other culturally defined transition points which are volitional, interactively generated, and physiologically less prominent. A woman's irreversible fall occurs through her addiction to earthly pleasures some time after defloration: at least one act of intercourse predates the fall. A man experiences his uplifting when he perceives of himself, his community, and Allah in proper relation: that moment of insightfulness pushes him to regulate (but not deny) his sexual impulses. Neither male nor female turns his or her back on natural sexual functioning according to the schema; instead each engages in a volitional decision-making process regarding it.

This convoluted mix of "natural" and "cultural," of spontaneous and volitional, helps give the lie to any simple male-cultural, female-natural formulation. Rather, the Taroudannt discourse takes as its foundation the belief that male and female both share in the "natural" and the "cultural." Indeed, each sex takes its turn according to the developmental scheme. The male sex is represented as moving from the "natural" to the "cultural" at the same time that the female sex moves from the "cultural" to the "natural." The two tendencies co-occur, a circumstance which is in keeping with the ideology's essential complementarity and dynamism. Moreover, while women may be deemed the more "natural" sex in the sense that it is the "natural" which women are believed ultimately to exhibit, men can also be perceived as more "natural," for they are born ruled by their instinctual desires, and their later lives consist of a continuing struggle against them. In fact, women can be said to display an almost certain virtue during virginity, while the attainment of a culturally defined positive sociality remains ever unsure over the course of men's lives.

The activity of both sexes as each generates its own and the other's development provides its contrast to a Western differentiation of male and female in terms of becoming and being. De Beauvoir (1949: 584) notes that "harmony is one of the keys to the feminine universe; it implies a stationary perfection" (1949: 584), with the corresponding male-associated concepts being action and movement. The distinction obviously carries with it a more positive valuation of males in a society that deifies progress. In the Moroccan system, by contrast, both male and female existences are developmental, both sexes emerge as active as well as responsive, and both are involved in becoming, albeit from opposing directions. Developmental thrust, rather than development or lack of it, becomes the primary criterion for how men and women are evaluated and viewed.

COGNITIVE MODELS
AND WOMEN'S SUBORDINATION

The issue of women's subordination has also been approached symbolically in a somewhat different vein, namely that if humankind shows its greater-than-animality through a capacity to symbolize—to imbue objects, relationships, and events with meanings that are more elaborate than their immediate attributes imply— then the measure of any group's humanness lies in the intricacy of its symbolic models, and the measure of that group's capacity to regulate human relations in a non-animal way lies in its facility or command over that symbolic (or "cultural," as some would term it) realm. The more intensively symboling group thus is likely to be seen as superior and thereby becomes a primary candidate for wielding authority and power.

Ortner (1974) again forwards this stance most explicitly. She posits that women's "psychic structure" is different from men's in that women display a "relative concreteness" as opposed to men's "relative abstractness" (1974: 81). Women's models, she argues, are more direct, more rooted in personal relations, and more unmediated, for the relationship that forms their prime foundation is a highly personalized one—the mother-daughter relationship—from which women learn how females should relate to the world through concrete examples to be imitated, rather than as abstract principles that are passed on, as mothers pass on to their sons principles about male behavior, orally or by implication. Moreover, it is not only the social scientist who recognizes that men's and women's representations differ. Women, like men, also see the more natural bent of their social models, says Ortner, and so are apt to conclude that women think in a less cultural way and so are inferior.

S. Ardener (1975) and E. Ardener (1972; 1975) also assert that women's cognitive models of the world are structurally different from men's. They, however, avoid the conclusion that this constitutes one reason why women are judged inferior and are subordinated in most societies. Rather, the Ardeners affirm that it is the reason why anthropologists (who presumably are drawn to the "cultural") are less interested in them. S. Ardener (1975: xiii), following E. Ardener, asserts that while both men and women hold deep, largely unconscious models which define the underlying continuities of life, women's "categories of society at the surface level of events" are more fragmentary. At that level, women's models, they say, are incompletely articulated and less neatly bounded than men's. One result, says E. Ardener (1972: 139) is that women often perceive their place in the world ambiguously: they "will not necessarily provide a model for society as a unit that will contain both men and themselves. They may indeed provide a model in which women and nature are outside men and society."

The Moroccanist must take issue with these hypotheses on several counts. One concerns paradigmatic form, another concerns women's capacity to communicate, and yet a third involves content origins. With regard to form, Moroccan men's and women's models, as revealed through several kinds of discourse, have a similar structure which displays its particular mix of abstractness and concreteness. This parallelism is especially apparent in the shared developmental framework, which, being largely unconscious, might be said to exist at Ardener's "deep" level, but is also evident in the narrower, more conscious "surface" level models which men and women propound. These pairings of "deep" and "surface" models, one male and one female, differ only in content, so that women are at no technical "disadvantage when wishing to express matters of particular concern to them" (S. Ardener 1975: viii f.). Indeed Moroccan women comprise a highly articulate group, although they sometimes opt to speak only among themselves. Nor, as the Taroudannt data remind us, do women necessarily accept the content of the models that men provide. The creative origins of the shared developmental framework are, of course, unknown, so that no one can know whether or not men formulated and women accepted them; but women's "surface" model of maleness demonstrates that women often reject men's conceptualizations. Ortner, S. Ardener, and E. Ardener portray women as acquiescing to the male-held symbol system that subordinates them, whereas Taroudannt women forward their own ideas in protest.

The Taroudannt data contribute to a growing literature which shows that women's symbolic models are often different from men's in terms of their valuations of men and women. In some societies, women value themselves more highly than men value them (Strathern 1972); in other societies, women value men less than men value themselves (Murphy and Murphy 1974). Whatever the particular combination of beliefs, however, women in many societies do not leave the validations of their subordination unchallenged, a fact which imparts political tension and often provides a potential for change in the male-female relational realm.

OTHER INTERLINKAGES

The close study of the Moroccan case thus reminds us that summary generalizing principles about symbol systems often do violence to the complexity of the phenomena that they attempt to subsume. A careful consideration of the Moroccan case points to a similar conclusion regarding theories about the underpinnings of sexual inequality. The incidence of sexually inegalitarian systems, and hence also the maintenance or rejection of them, has most often been linked to the action systems of economics, politics, and/or social organization, to the relative exclusion of the belief systems that are operative along with them. Men's assumption of control over private property (Sacks 1974), the breakdown of female work groups (Johnson and Johnson 1975), the impact of Western colonialism (Leacock 1972) have each and in combination been designated as crucial in the subordination of women. I do not want here to discuss the merits of each hypothesis, except to point out that the Moroccan case indeed demonstrates the importance of each of these elements in limiting women's life options. Rather, I wish to stress that ideology must be moved from the niche of epiphenomenon if women's subordination is to be more completely understood. In underscoring that point, I will, briefly, in closing, consider how these action systems have their own ideological aspects and how behavior and belief in these spheres affect and are affected by the belief system already presented. It is not the primacy of belief that I argue, but rather the need to redress the balance by considering the complex role of belief in sexual politics.

Let us begin ostensibly outside the belief sphere with a rather apparent social-organizational shift that is occurring in Taroudannt, one which has attacted the attention of numerous social scientists when it has occurred in other regions of the world and one which Taroudannt residents themselves acknowledge: the loosening or deterioration of what have been called "female support" groups. (The term itself is a misleading one, for these groups often serve quite as frequently as mechanisms for women's control.) Data from various societies indicate that groups of women, when corporately organized to some degree, can provide their members with power in male-female relations that they might otherwise lack. Groups of Barabaig women in East Africa inflict injury upon men and destroy men's property when men wrong women: the female group seizes a defensive and offensive initiative, and men reckon with that fact, it constituting one of women's recognized recourses and rights (Klima 1964). Mundurucu women in South America join together during the manioc pressing: on these occasions, they exchange information, bolster one another's self-images, and present an occasional united front against their men (Murphy and Murphy 1974). And women of a Taroudannt street neighborhood, although rather loosely joined into a voluntary network that is dependent upon the mobility which household heads accord, exhibit similar power by virtue of those same-sexed contacts. The women of a Taroudannt street can and do support one another and occasionally protect one another by providing cover for each other's pilfering and sexual transgressions.

The existence of intensely interacting female neighbors provides Taroudannt women with a strategic alternative as they seek to lessen their vulnerability in encounters with men. One might question, then, what the likely effect upon the power of women, and upon male-female relations generally, is of forces that tend to isolate women from their neighbors and which encourage women to act more independently and atomistically. The question is a real one in the minds of Roudaniyin, who see these forces as already impinging, and their responses reveal a complex blend of hopes and fears. For women, there are perceived potential losses but also perceived possible gains. As women's neighborhood involvements diminish, their ability to camouflage illicit behavior is reduced. A robe obtained from a male admirer can no longer be disguised as a loan from a neighbor; nor can a stolen sugar cone be so easily passed on to a buyer in the street. As one Taroudannt woman asserted, openly recognizing the importance of such strategies: "How, without neighbors and family, can a woman get hold of her rightful portion?" (Women sometimes call pocket money taken from husbands their "rightful portion" or ḥaqq). And yet separation and isolation also provide advantages for women, to which men frequently allude in their moments of pessimism. The isolated woman is less supervised, and this, in its own way, can encourage illicit behavior. After all, Roudaniyin affirm, neighbors are the community's most trusted witnesses and are believed to serve in that capacity before earthly judges and Allah. Advocates of a tight control system thus often lament that "the street is gone," fearing that residents, especially female ones, will more easily go beyond the bounds of propriety.

The breakdown of neighborhood solidarity has familiar economic and ideological correlates, perhaps the most important ideological one being the rise of what has sometimes been labeled individualism. On the economic front, family members now frequently find work as wage laborers, and neighborhood and extended family work groups, once important as organizing structures for both males and females, are becoming things of the past. Emigrant workers, who are frequently found in the Taroudannt region, carry this individualistic note to an even higher pitch: cutting themselves off from their acquaintances for substantial time periods, they bring considerable wealth back to their home regions. Their presence as such is generally regarded as an asset. And yet the enthusiasm of home folk about them tends not to be total, for emigrant laborers are often seen as working toward a narrower self-interest and so not doing enough for kinfolk and friends. Some Roudaniyin regard this as a particularly Arab-urban tendency: they say that emigrant workers from the city all too often discourage the hiring of relatives and friends, for they wish to be better than their homefolk. This stands in sharp contrast to the motivations that are imputed to Berber workers from the city's environs: the Berber is said to encourage recruitment of kinsmen and acquaintances, evincing pride in their success.

These shifting economic and social patterns carry with them yet other perceptions which themselves are coming under review. Roudaniyin are not only expressing hopes and fears that neighborhoods will break down or that workers are moving toward a narrower definition of self-interest: they are also voicing their support or misgivings for a new concept of selfhood, a revised perception of propriety, and a changed notion of sociality that are associated with these two. The more long-standing notions are key to a specifically Moroccan attitude about maleness and femaleness as well as to Moroccan social and economic philosophy, and pressure upon them can affect male-female relations, this time from a more explicitly ideological direction.

As Geertz notes (1975), the attempt to understand cultural concepts of personhood—and for our purposes, cultural concepts of sexual personhood—is a difficult undertaking, for notions of personhood are highly complex and vary considerably from society to society. For the Taroudannt case, one might usefully isolate several counterthemes in the notion of the person, among them one which Geertz has identified as "Moroccan" and one which he has designated "Western," both of which seem to exist in at least rudimentary form in Taroudannt society. According to the "Moroccan" perception, personhood is socially embedded. It unfolds interactionally, so that personality or character varies rather flexibly from relationship to relationship. The self defines itself contextually. By contrast, the "Western" perception stresses the person as an isolate. According to this view, the person is a "bounded, unique, more or less integrated motivational and cognitive universe . . . set contrastively against other such wholes and against a social and natural background" (Geertz 1975: 48). Given this view, isolation rather than interaction becomes the soundest "Western" route to discovering the self.

The two views are extremes, of course, and Moroccan perceptions of sexual selfhood certainly contain aspects of each. Beliefs about the internal predispositions of the two sexes—the male-positive and female-negative developmental trajectories—accord with the "individuated whole" notion, for they emerge more nearly as internally arising attributes. But these potentialities also require male-female interaction, and social interaction more generally, in order to be actualized: an act of defloration, for example, puts a virgin on the route to sexual awareness and excess; a familial life of worry and hardship provides a favorable context for the shaping of a morally responsible man. In this sense, a precondition for loosing the internal developmental dynamic is social embeddedness.

If one must pinpoint the stronger tendency in the Taroudannt sexual ideological scheme, the relational view of the self seems to predominate. Each sex forms an integral part of the other's social and spiritual environment. Indeed, valued characteristics are inversely distributed, qualitatively and quantitatively, between the male and the female. The origin myths involving Adam and Eve underscore the primacy of the intertwining and the interdependence. Adam and Eve move in opposing moral directions when together, but even when separate and untainted, they share one primal drive, the urge to interact.

This relational view contrasts with the greater individualism evident in many sexual ideologies in the West. In Morocco, a woman is a virgin deflowered: an interactive act determines a female's sexual identity and social status. In the West, a woman more nearly attains womanhood by virtue of her physiological development and age. Indeed, femaleness and maleness can be comfortably defined and discussed in Western terms without any recognition of the other sex, for example, in terms of a person's chromosomal makeup.

Pressure for change in present-day Roudaniy representations of male and female thus is being felt directly through confrontation with Western images and more indirectly through the impact of economic, political, and social forces that have ideological correlates and implications. But pressure for maintenance is also being marshaled along numerous paths, some of them again ideological. The demise of the street as a social and economic unit takes on a more dangerous mien through its association with the image of the licentious woman suddenly loosed; the argument calls to mind considerable felt dangers for both men and women. The deepening involvement of Moroccans in the European labor force is sometimes represented as narrowly beneficial but ultimately corrupting: the Berber, less civilized and less responsive according to the Roudaniy view, emerges in some Roudaniyin's eyes as the only likely candidate for economic involvement, with its submission to European cultural patterns. The association, this time critical of the West, gains through Roudaniyin's long-standing use of the Berber-Arab contrast in sustaining their self-images. The attraction of the West, which looms as rich, powerful, but only limitedly known to most Roudaniyin, is countered by the image of daughters, sisters, and wives unveiled and scantily clad in Western clothes. Belief in women's powerful sexuality and in men's vulnerability transforms the scene into one that augurs chaos and promiscuity.

The Arab-Muslim sexual belief system has long provided important subject matter for these and other debates. Europeans and Arab-Muslims have long engaged in a dialogue about the relative worth of their cultural traditions, with male-female relations being forwarded as apt illustrations by both sides. Advocates of "modernization" and proponents of "traditionalism," inside and outside the Arab-Muslim community, have long found in the sphere of male-female relations one occasion to project their hopes and fears and to argue about the future direction of the society. The subject matter of male-female relations is a prime debating point in each of these arenas, however, largely because of the artfulness of certain logically prior discourses: those between Arab-Muslim males and females, males and males, and females and females about the two sexes' weaknesses and capabilities and hence also about the appropriateness of a system of males dominance and female subordination. As the Taroudannt case shows, there is drama in these exchanges, for they involve a notion of women's efficacy confronting women's denigration, of acquiescence mingling with protest, in a context in which the subordinate sex is often left to supervise itself because it can be only insufficiently supervised from outside. There is occasion for resistance and with it insights as to how resistance can be muted through the use of an ideology of women's subordination that is structured and presented captivatingly.

BIBLIOGRAPHY

Andrae, Tor. 1960. *Mohammed: The Man and His Faith.* New York: Harper and Row.

Antoun, Richard T. 1968. "Arab Muslim Villages: A Study of the Accommodation of Traditions." *American Anthropologist,* 70: 671–97.

Arberry, A. J. 1955. *The Koran Interpreted.* New York: Macmillan.

Ardener, Edwin. 1972. "Belief and the Problem of Women." In J. S. La Fontaine, ed, *The Interpretation of Ritual.* London: Tavistock.

—— 1975. "The Problem Revisited." In Shirley Ardener, ed, *Perceiving Women.* New York: Halsted Press.

Ardener, Shirley. 1975. "Introduction." In Shirley Ardener, ed, *Perceiving Women.* New York: Halsted Press.

Asad, Talal. 1974. "Two European Images of Non-European Rule." In Talal Asad, ed., *Anthropology and the Colonial Encounter.* London: Ithaca Press.

Bachofen, J. J. 1967. *Myth, Religion, and Mother Right.* Translated by L Ralph Manheim. Princeton: Princeton University Press.

de Beauvoir, Simone. 1949. *The Second Sex.* New York: Bantam.

—— 1970. *La Vieillesse.* Paris: Gallimard.

Bettelheim, Bruno. 1976. *The Uses of Enchantment.* New York: Alfred Knopf.

Bousquet, G.-H. 1958. *Abrége de la loi musulmane selon le rite de l'Imam Malek.* Alger: La Maison des Livres.

Buret, M.-T. 1947. "Comparison folklorique, deux contes marocains et contes de Grimm." *Hesperis,* 34: 463–64.

Chabbi, Begacem Karoui. 1974. "Reflexion sur la condition juridique de la femme arabo-musulmane, matriarcat et concubinage." *Revue Juridique et Politique Indépendence et Coopération,* 4: 558–67.

Chodorow, Nancy. 1974. "Family Structure and Feminine Personality." In Michelle Z. Rosaldo and Louise Lamphere, eds., *Women, Culture, and Society.* Stanford: Stanford University Press.

Colomer, André. 1963. *Droit musulman: les personnes, la famille.* Rabat: Éditions la Porte.

Coulson, Noel J. 1966. *Conflicts and Tensions in Islamic Jurisprudence.* Chicago: University of Chicago Press.

Dwyer, Daisy Hilse. 1977. "Bridging the Gap Between the Sexes in Moroccan Legal Practice." In Alice Schlegel, ed, *Sexual Stratification: A Cross-Cultural View.* New York: Columbia University Press.

—— 1978. "Women, Sufism, and Decision-Making in Moroccan Islam." In Nikki Keddie and Lois Beck, eds, *Muslim Women.* Cambridge: Harvard University Press.

Faithorn, Elizabeth. 1975. "The Concept of Pollution Among the Káfe of the Papuan New Guinea Highlands." In Rayna R. Reiter, ed, *Toward an Anthropology of Women.* New York: Monthly Review Press.

Fanon, Frantz. 1966. "L'Algérie se dévoile." In *Sociologie d'une révolution.* Paris: Maspero.

Friedl, Ernestine. 1975. *Women and Men: An Anthropologist's View.* New York: Holt, Rinehart, and Winston.

Gaudry, Mathea. 1928. *La Femme chaouia de l'Aurès.* Paris: Guethner.

Geertz, Clifford. 1975. "On the Nature of Anthropological Understanding." *American Scientist,* 63: 47–53.

Granqvist, Hilma. 1931. *Marriage Conditions in a Palestinian Village.* Helsingfors: Commentationes Humanarum Litterarum.

Griaule, Marcel. 1947. "Nouvelles recherches sur la notion de personne chez les Dogons (Soudan Francais)." *Journal de Psychologie Normale et Pathologique,* 40: 425–31.

Jameson, Frederic. 1972. *The Prison-House of Language*. Princeton: Princeton University Press.

Johnson, Orna R., and Allen Johnson. 1975. "Male/Female Relations and the Organization of Work in a Machiguenga Community." *American Ethnologist* 2(4): 634–48.

Katchadourian, Herant A., and Donald T. Lunde. 1975. *Fundamentals of Human Sexuality*. New York: Holt, Rinehart, and Winston.

Klima, George. 1964. "Jural Relations Between the Sexes Among the Barabaig." *Africa*, 34: 9–20.

Lacoste-Dujardin, Camille. 1973. "Littérature orale populaire maghrebine." *Annuaire de l'Afrique du Nord*, 12: 249–57.

Lane, E. W. 1908. *Manners and Customs of the Modern Egyptians*. London: J. M. Dent and Sons.

Laroui, Abdallah. 1967. *L'Idéologie arabe contemporaine*. Paris: Maspero.

Leacock, Eleanor Burke. 1972. "Introduction to Frederick Engels." In Eleanor Burke Leacock, ed, *The Origin of the Family, Private Property and the State*. New York: International Publishers.

Levy, Reuben. 1965. *The Social Structure of Islam*. London: Cambridge University Press.

Mahdi, Muhsin. 1964. *Ibn Khaldun's Philosophy of History*. Chicago: Phoenix.

Martin, M. Kay, and Barbara Voorhies. 1975. *The Female of the Species*. New York: Columbia University Press.

Mead, Margaret. 1928. *Coming of Age in Samoa*. New York: William Morrow.

—— 1935. *Sex and Temperament*. New York: William Morrow.

Mernissi, Fatima. 1975. *Beyond the Veil: Male-Female Dynamics in a Modern Muslim Society*. New York: John Wiley and Sons.

Morales, Angel Flores. 1948. *Atlas-Sus-Dra*. Madrid: Instituto de Estudios Africanos.

Murphy, Yolanda, and Robert F. Murphy. 1974. *Women of the Forest*. New York: Columbia University Press.

Ortner, Sherry B. 1974. "Is Female to Male as Nature is to Culture?" In Michelle Z. Rosaldo and Louise Lamphere, eds., *Women, Culture, and Society*. Stanford: Stanford University Press.

Pruvost, Lucie. 1974. "Condition juridique, politique et sociale de la femme. Le 9e Congress de l'IDEF." *IBLA*, 134: 349–64.

Rosaldo, Michelle Zimbalist. 1975. "Man the Hunter and Woman: Meta-
phors for the Sexes in Ilongot Magical Spells." In Roy Willis, ed.,
The Interpretation of Symbolism. New York: John Wiley and Sons.

Rosenfeld, Henry. 1960. "On Determinants of the Status of Arab Village
Women." *Man,* 60: 66–70.

Sacks, Karen. 1974. "Engels Revisited: Women, the Organization of
Production and Private Property." In Michelle Z. Rosaldo and
Louise Lamphere, eds., *Women, Culture, and Society.* Stanford:
Stanford University Press.

Sammari, Mohamed Salah Rached. 1974. "Reflexion sur la condition de
la femme en droit musulman." *Revue Juridique et Politique Indépendence et Coopération,* 4: 548–57.

Scelles-Millie, J. 1970. *Contes arabes du Maghreb.* Paris: Maisonneuve
et Larose.

Silverman, Sydel. 1967. "The Life Crisis as a Clue to Social Functions."
Anthropological Quarterly, 40: 127–38.

Smith, Margaret. 1928. *Rabiʻa the Mystic and Her Fellow-Saints in Islam.*
Cambridge: Cambridge University Press.

Strathern, Marilyn. 1972. *Women In Between: Female Roles in a Male
World.* New York: Seminar Press.

Vinogradov, Amal. 1974. "French Colonialism as Reflected in the Male-
Female Interaction in Morocco." *Transactions of the New York
Academy of Sciences,* ser. II, 36: 192–99.

Westermarck, Edward. 1914. *Marriage Ceremonies in Morocco.* London: Macmillan.

—— 1926. *Ritual and Belief in Morocco.* London: Macmillan.

—— 1930. *Wit and Wisdom in Morocco.* London: George Routledge.

INDEX

189